Romantic Style

JUL   2007

KIRKLAND

Romantic Style

Knits and Crochet to Wear or Display

Jennie Atkinson

with Lois Daykin, Kim Hargreaves,
Sharon Miller, and Martin Storey

For my lovely mother, Valda, and
to the memory of my father, Ivor.

First published in 2006 by
Rowan Yarns
Green Lane Mill
Holmfirth
West Yorkshire
HD9 2DX

Editor Sally Harding
Designer Nicky Downes
Special photography John Heseltine
Stylist Emma Freemantle
Pattern writer Penny Hill
Pattern checker Stella Smith

ISBN-10: 1-56477-715-4
ISBN-13: 978-1-56477-715-7

Printed in Singapore

CONTENTS

Introduction 6
Gallery of Designs 8

Out and About 10
Cotton Camisole 12
Beaded Cape 18
Butterfly Dress 22
Lace Blouse 28
Beaded Jacket 32
Beaded Shrug 38
Chevron Lace Top 42

Home Comforts 48
Bed Jacket 50
Dressing Gown 54
Diamond Throw 60
Lacy Bed Socks 64
Hanger Covers 68
Rose Button Cushion 72
Buttoned Flower Bolster 76

Little Extras 80
Crochet Necklace 84
Crochet Choker 85
Crochet Belt 86

Crochet Shawl 88
Crochet Motif Bag 92
Lace Shawl 96
Button Crochet Belt 100
Crochet Cap 104
Buttoned Bag 108

Techniques 112
Working crochet in rounds 114
Crochet motifs 116
Simple crochet edgings 120
Following knitting and
crochet patterns 122
Abbreviations and glossary 125

Yarn Information 126
Yarn Addresses 127
Acknowledgments 128

Introduction

The wonderful thing about knitting and crochet is that you can create any look you want by the choice of yarn, color, stitch pattern, and applied decoration. The pieces I have designed for this book conjure a romantic, delicate, feminine look for you and your home. As well as my own designs, I have included work by some wonderfully talented designers that I believe fit in with the romantic style of the book.

There are designs for knitters of all skills. For the experienced knitter, there is the Butterfly Dress (see page 22), and for the experienced crocheter, the gorgeous Crochet Shawl designed by Kim Hargreaves (see page 89). Some lace stitches can be hard for the inexperienced knitter to follow, but I hope that with these designs I have shown that a lacy look can be achieved with the use of simple lace stitches and pretty lace edgings. And with the addition of buttons and beads, even a novice knitter can achieve the desired effect.

For the knitter who has never crocheted before, here's a chance to try it out. There are instructions for simple crochet edgings on pages 120 and 121. Making these is an easy way to give an attractive finish to any garment. Once you have mastered the basic stitches, you can progress to the simple crochet accessories in the book— necklaces, belts, a cap, and a gorgeous shawl.

Most of all, I encourage you to try to experiment. Changing the yarn color of the Bed Jacket or Dressing Gown to darker shades, will give garments that can be worn as daywear (see pages 50 and 54). The edging in one pattern could be used in another—for example, knit the hanger cover edging using Rowan's luxurious Kidsilk Haze and sew it onto the Hooded Shrug as an alternative to the beaded crocheted edge. Or substitute the buttons and beads used for various designs with ones of your own choice and end up with completely unique garments of your own!

I hope you will see that with a little confidence you can create your own wonderfully romantic pieces, using the ideas provided in this book.

Jennie Atkinson

GALLERY OF DESIGNS

Here are all the knitting and crochet designs included in this book. You can make them in the colors shown or choose your own, if you prefer. However, if you change the yarn type as well as the color, you must always work a gauge square first to check that the measurements will be correct (see further information on pages 122–127).

Out and About

Cotton Camisole
by Jennie Atkinson
pages 12–17

Beaded Cape
by Jennie Atkinson
pages 18–21

Butterfly Dress
by Jennie Atkinson
pages 22–27

Lace Blouse
by Jennie Atkinson
pages 28–31

Beaded Jacket
by Kim Hargreaves
pages 32–37

Beaded Shrug
by Jennie Atkinson
pages 38–41

Chevron Lace Top
by Kim Hargreaves
pages 42–47

Home Comforts

Bed Jacket
by Jennie Atkinson
pages 50–53

Dressing Gown
by Jennie Atkinson
pages 54–59

Diamond Throw
by Jennie Atkinson
pages 60–63

Lacy Bed Socks
by Jennie Atkinson
pages 64–67

Hanger Covers
by Jennie Atkinson
pages 68–71

Rose Button Cushion
by Lois Daykin
pages 72–75

**Buttoned Flower
Bolster** by Lois Daykin
pages 76–79

Little Extras

Crochet Necklace
by Jennie Atkinson
page 84

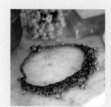

Crochet Choker
by Jennie Atkinson
page 85

Crochet Belt
by Jennie Atkinson
page 86

Crochet Shawl
by Kim Hargreaves
pages 88–91

Crochet Motif Bag
by Martin Storey
pages 92–95

Lace Shawl
by Sharon Miller
pages 96–99

Button Crochet Belt
by Jennie Atkinson
pages 100–103

Crochet Cap
by Kim Hargreaves
pages 104–107

Buttoned Bag
by Kim Hargreaves
pages 108–111

Out and About

Cotton Camisole • Beaded Cape

Butterfly Dress • Lace Blouse

Beaded Jacket • Beaded Shrug

Chevron Lace Top

Cotton Camisole

This is the ideal top to wear either under a suit in the fall or winter, or on its own in summer. Knitted in a crisp, mercerized cotton yarn, it has a lovely neat finish, with attractive bowed shaping along the bottom edge. The fitted bra-top makes it ideal to wear with nothing underneath it. Match it up with the Lace Blouse on page 29 for a really pretty twinset.

COTTON CAMISOLE by Jennie Atkinson

SIZES

	XS	S	M	L	XL	
To fit bust	32	34	36	38	40	in.
	81	86	91	97	102	cm

For actual size, see diagram below.
(**Note:** Width given on diagram is for under-bust measurement.)

YARN

3 [4, 4, 5, 5] balls of Jaeger *Siena* (50g/ 1³/₄oz) in main color **MC** (White 401 was used here)
Scrap of cotton fingering-weight (4-ply-weight) waste yarn in a contrasting color

NEEDLES

Pair of size 2 (2.75mm) knitting needles
Two size 2 (2.75mm) double-pointed knitting needles

EXTRAS

Elastic knitting thread

GAUGE

30 sts and 40 rows to 4 in./10cm measured over stockinette stitch using size 2 (2.75mm) knitting needles.

BACK

Using size 2 (2.75mm) needles and waste yarn in a contrasting color, cast on 110 [118, 126, 134, 142] sts.
Beg with a K row, work 2 rows in St st. Break off waste yarn and change to yarn MC.
Beg with a K row, work 6 rows in St st, ending with RS facing for next row.
Next row (picot row) (RS): K1, *yo, K2tog, rep from * to last st, K1.
Beg with a P row, work 7 rows in St st, ending with RS facing for next row.
Next row (RS): Fold up hem along picot row so that WS are tog and first row in yarn MC is aligned at back of work with sts on left needle, then insert right needle knitwise through first st on left needle and through top of corresponding st in first row in yarn MC and K these sts tog, cont along row in same way knitting through both layers at same time.
110 [118, 126, 134, 142] sts.
(**Note:** When picking up hem sts, make sure waste yarn remains outside hem so that it can be removed later.)
Shaped hem
Next row (WS): P74 [79, 84, 89, 94], then bring yarn to opposite side of work between 2 needles, slip next st purlwise onto right needle, take yarn back to original side of work and slip slipped st back onto left needle—called ***wrap next st***—, turn work (leaving 36 [39, 42, 45, 48] sts on left needle unworked).
Next row: K38 [40, 42, 44, 46], wrap next st, then turn work (leaving 36 [39, 42, 45, 48] sts on left needle unworked).
Next row: P50 [53, 56, 59, 62], wrap next st, turn work.
Next row: K62 [66, 70, 74, 78], wrap next st, turn work.
Next row: P74 [79, 84, 89, 94], wrap next st, turn work.
Next row: K86 [92, 98, 104, 110], wrap next st, turn work.
Next row: P to end.
Next row: K to end (all sts).
Beg with a P row, work even in St st for 3 more rows.
Cont in St st, dec one st at each end of next row, then on every foll 6th row 5 times. 98 [106, 114, 122, 130] sts.**
Cont in St st until work measures 9 [9½, 9½, 9¾, 9¾] in./23 [24, 24, 25, 25]cm from picot edge at center of back, ending with RS facing for next row.
Using yarn and elastic knitting thread held tog, work 4 rows in K1, P1 rib.
Bind off in rib.

LOWER FRONT

Work as for back to **.
Cont in St st until there are 30 fewer rows than back to beg of rib, ending with RS facing for next row.
Shape top of front
Cont in St st, bind off 16 [18, 20, 22, 24] sts at beg next 4 rows, then 5 sts at beg next 6 rows, ending with RS facing for next row. 4 sts.
Next row: (K2tog) twice.

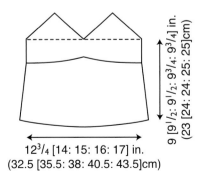

12³/₄ [14: 15: 16: 17] in.
(32.5 [35.5: 38: 40.5: 43.5]cm)

9 [9¹/₂: 9¹/₂: 9³/₄: 9³/₄] in. (23 [24: 24: 25: 25]cm)

Next row: P2tog and fasten off.

RIGHT FRONT CUP

Each bra-top cup of front is worked sideways, starting at center front.
Using size 2 (2.75mm) needles and yarn MC, cast on 15 sts.
Row 1 (RS): K to end.
Row 2: P to end.
Row 3 (picot row): K2, *yo, K2tog, rep from * to last st, K1.
Row 4: P to end.
Row 5: K2, yo, K to last st, K into front and back of last st to inc one st.
Row 6: P to end.
Row 7: K2, yo, K to end.
Row 8: P into front and back of first st to inc one st, P to end.
Row 9: K2, yo, K to end.
Row 10: P to end.
Rep last 6 rows 4 [4, 4, 5, 5] times, then first 0 [2, 4, 0, 2] of these rows again, ending with RS facing for next row.
40 [42, 44, 45, 47] sts.
Next row (RS): K2, yo, K to last 2 sts, turn work.
Next row: P to end.
(**Note:** When turning on these rows, sts are not wrapped—holes formed are part of design.)
Next row: K2, yo, K to last 4 sts, turn work.
Next row: P to end.
Next row: K2, yo, K to last 6 sts, turn work.
Next row: P to end.
Next row: K2, yo, K to last 8 sts, turn work.
Next row: P to end.
Next row: K2, yo, K to last 10 sts, turn work.
Next row: P to end.
Next row: K2, yo, K to last 12 sts, turn work.

Next row: P to end.
Next row: K2, yo, K to last 14 sts, turn work.
Next row: P to end.
S, M, L, and XL sizes only
Next row: K2, yo, K to last 16 sts, turn work.
Next row: P to end.
M, L, and XL sizes only
Next row: K2, yo, K to last 18 sts, turn work.
Next row: P to end.
L and XL sizes only
Next row: K2, yo, K to last 20 sts, turn work.
Next row: P to end.
XL size only
Next row: K2, yo, K to last 22 sts, turn work.
Next row: P to end.
Next row: K2, skp, K to last 20 sts, turn work.
Next row: P to end.
L and XL sizes only
Next row: K2, skp, K to last 18 sts, turn work.
Next row: P to end.
M, L, and XL sizes only
Next row: K2, skp, K to last 16 sts, turn work.
Next row: P to end.
S, M, L, and XL sizes only
Next row: K2, skp, K to last 14 sts, turn work.
Next row: P to end.
All sizes
Next row: K2, skp, K to last 12 sts, turn work.
Next row: P to end.
Next row: K2, skp, K to last 10 sts, turn work.
Next row: P to end.
Next row: K2, skp, K to last 8 sts, turn work.

Next row: P to end.
Next row: K2, skp, K to last 6 sts, turn work.
Next row: P to end.
Next row: K2, skp, K to last 4 sts, turn work.
Next row: P to end.
Next row: K2, skp, K to last 2 sts, turn work.
Next row: P to end.
Next row: K2, skp, K to end.
40 [42, 44, 45, 47] sts.
Next row: P to end.
Rep last 2 rows until 24 [24, 24, 23, 23] sts rem.
Bind off.

LEFT FRONT CUP

Using size 2 (2.75mm) needles and yarn MC, cast on 15 sts.
Row 1 (RS): K to end.
Row 2: P to end.
Row 3 (picot row): K1, *yo, K2tog, rep from * to last 2 sts, K2.
Row 4: P to end.
Row 5: K into front and back of first st to inc one st, K to last 2 sts, yo, K2.
Row 6: P to end.
Row 7: K to last 2 sts, yo, K2.
Row 8: P to last st, P into front and back of last st to inc one st.
Row 9: K to last 2 sts, yo, K2.
Row 10: P to end.
Rep last 6 rows 4 [4, 4, 5, 5] times, then first 0 [2, 4, 0, 2] of these rows again, ending with RS facing for next row.
40 [42, 44, 45, 47] sts.
Next row (RS): K to last 2 sts, yo, K2.
Next row: P to last 2 sts, turn work.
(**Note:** When turning on these rows, sts are not wrapped—the holes formed are part of design.)
Next row: K to last 2 sts, yo, K2.
Next row: P to last 4 sts, turn work.

Next row: K to last 2 sts, yo, K2.
Next row: P to last 6 sts, turn work.
Next row: K to last 2 sts, yo, K2.
Next row: P to last 8 sts, turn work.
Next row: K to last 2 sts, yo, K2.
Next row: P to last 10 sts, turn work.
Next row: K to last 2 sts, yo, K2.
Next row: P to last 12 sts, turn work.
Next row: K to last 2 sts, yo, K2.
Next row: P to last 14 sts, turn work.

S, M, L, and XL sizes only
Next row: K to last 2 sts, yo, K2.
Next row: P to last 16 sts, turn work.

M, L, and XL sizes only
Next row: K to last 2 sts, yo, K2.
Next row: P to last 18 sts, turn work.

L and XL sizes only
Next row: K to last 2 sts, yo, K2.
Next row: P to last 20 sts, turn work.

XL size only
Next row: K to last 2 sts, yo, K2.
Next row: P to last 22 sts, turn work.
Next row: K to last 4 sts, K2tog tbl, K2.
Next row: P to last 20 sts, turn work.

L and XL sizes only
Next row: K to last 4 sts, K2tog tbl, K2.
Next row: P to last 18 sts, turn work.

M, L, and XL sizes only
Next row: K to last 4 sts, K2tog tbl, K2.
Next row: P to last 16 sts, turn work.

S, M, L, and XL sizes only
Next row: K to last 4 sts, K2tog tbl, K2.
Next row: P to last 14 sts, turn work.

All sizes
Next row: K to last 4 sts, K2tog tbl, K2.
Next row: P to last 12 sts, turn work.
Next row: K to last 4 sts, K2tog tbl, K2.
Next row: P to last 10 sts, turn work.
Next row: K to last 4 sts, K2tog tbl, K2.
Next row: P to last 8 sts, turn work.
Next row: K to last 4 sts, K2tog tbl, K2.
Next row: P to last 6 sts, turn work.

Next row: K to last 4 sts, K2tog tbl, K2.
Next row: P to last 4 sts, turn work.
Next row: K to last 4 sts, K2tog tbl, K2.
Next row: P to last 2 sts, turn work.
Next row: K to last 4 sts, K2tog tbl, K2.
40 [42, 44, 45, 47] sts.
Next row: P to end.
Rep last 2 rows until 24 [24, 24, 23, 23] sts rem.
Bind off.

SHOULDER STRAPS (MAKE 2)
Using two size 2 (2.75mm) double-pointed needles, cast on 4 sts.
Row 1 (RS): K to end. Do not turn at end of row.
Row 2: With RS still facing, slide sts to beg of needle, then bring yarn across WS of work and K to end. Do not turn at end of row.
Rep row 2 until strap measures 13 [12½, 13, 13, 13½] in./33 [32, 33, 33, 34]cm or required length.
Break off yarn, thread end through sts, pull tight to gather and secure.

FINISHING
Remove waste yarn from hems.
Block then press pieces lightly on WS, following instructions on yarn label.
Sew together cast-on edges of left and right cups, using overcast stitch. Then sew cups to top of lower front, using backstitch. Sew front to back at side seams.
Sew one end of each strap to tip of V-shape on each cup; sew other end of strap to back on WS of ribbing, spacing them about 6 [6½, 6½, 6¾, 6¾] in./15.5 [16.5, 16.5, 17.5, 17.5]cm apart.

Beaded Cape

This cape looks very sophisticated but is, in fact, easy to knit. Worked in soft merino wool in stockinette stitch with knit-in shimmering glass beads, it is made in simple shaped panels that are stitched together later. Wear it as here with the Buttoned Crochet Belt on page 101 and you have the perfect party-time outfit.

BEADED CAPE by Jennie Atkinson

SIZES AND MEASUREMENTS

	XS–S	M–L	
To fit bust	32–34	36–38	in.
	81–86	91–97	cm

Knitted measurements

Length to shoulder	12	12	in.
	30	30	cm

YARN

3 [3] balls of Rowan *4-Ply Soft* (50g/
1¾oz) in desired shade (Whisper 370
was used here)

NEEDLES

Pair of size 3 (3.25mm) knitting needles
Two size 2 (2.75mm) double-pointed
knitting needles

EXTRAS

3mm round glass beads, approximately
1540 [1760], in a mixture of gold,
pewter, and clear (Rowan nos. 01005,
01006, and 01007)
24 in./60cm of 1 in./2.5cm wide
grosgrain ribbon

GAUGE

28 sts and 36 rows to 4 in./10cm
measured over stockinette stitch using
size 3 (3.25mm) needles.

SPECIAL ABBREVIATION

bead 1 = bring yarn to RS of work, slide
bead up next to st just worked, slip next
stitch purlwise from left needle to right
needle, and take yarn back to WS of
work, leaving bead sitting on RS of work
in front of slipped st.

PANELS

Thread 220 beads onto yarn.
Using size 3 (3.25mm) needles and
placing one bead between each st, cast
on 66 sts.
Place bead chart patt as foll:

Row 1 and all odd-numbered rows (WS):
P to end.
Row 2 (RS): K1, work across 64 sts of
row 2 of chart, K1.
Row 4: K1, work across 64 sts of row 4
of chart, K1.
These 4 rows set chart patt.
Cont in patt to end of chart, dec one st
at each end of next row and every foll
4th row. 48 sts.
Cont to dec one st at each end of every
4th row until 14 sts rem, ending with RS
facing for next row. Bind off.
This completes first panel.
Make 6 [7] more panels in same way.

CORD TIE

Using two size 2 (2.75mm) double-
pointed needles, cast on 3 sts.
Row 1 (RS): K into front and back of
each st. Do not turn at end of row. 6 sts.

Row 2: With RS still facing, slide sts to
beg of needle, then bring yarn across WS
of work and K to end. Do not turn at end
of row.
Rep row 2 until cord tie measures 39
[41] in./100 [105]cm from cast-on edge.
Next row: With RS still facing, slide sts
to beg of needle, then bring yarn across
WS of work and (K2tog) 3 times.
Thread yarn through 3 rem sts and
fasten off.

FINISHING

Sew panels together.
Cut grosgrain ribbon in half. Pin one
piece to back of each front edge, one
stitch in from edge, and sew in place,
turning a hem to WS at each end of
ribbon. Pin center neck edge of cape
to center of cord and sew cord to
neck edge.

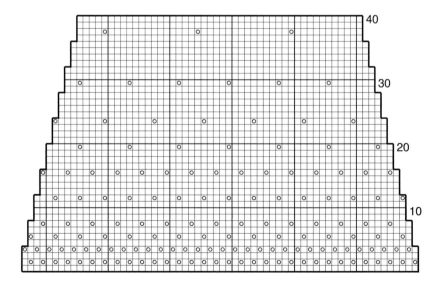

Key

□ K on RS, P on WS   ⊚ bead 1

Butterfly Dress

As the name suggests, this beautiful lacy beaded
dress would transform any average caterpillar
into a butterfly in seconds! Wear it over a silk
underslip—it is the ultimate in gossamer
lightness—and dance the night away. Knitted in
Rowan's exquisite mohair-and-silk Kidsilk Haze,
it has a tantalizing doubled lace hem.

BUTTERFLY DRESS by Jennie Atkinson

SIZES

	XS	S	M	L	XL	
To fit bust	32	34	36	38	40	in.
	81	86	91	97	102	cm

For actual size, see diagram below.
(**Note:** Lace stretches to fit.)

YARN

3 [3, 3, 3, 4] balls of Rowan *Kidsilk Haze* (25g/1oz) in main color **MC** and one ball in contrasting color **CC** (Majestic 589 was used here for MC and Smoke 605 for CC) Lightweight waste yarn in contrasting color

NEEDLES

Pair each of size 3 (3.25mm), size 7 (4.5mm), and size 8 (5mm) knitting needles

EXTRAS

3mm round glass beads, approximately 500, in copper (Rowan no. 01009)

3mm round glass beads, approximately 500, in pewter (Rowan no. 01006)

GAUGE

17 sts and 24 rows to 4 in./10cm measured over pattern using size 8 (5mm) needles.

SPECIAL ABBREVIATIONS

bead 1 = bring yarn to RS of work, slide bead up next to stitch just worked, slip next stitch purlwise from left needle to right needle, and take yarn back to WS of work, leaving bead sitting on RS of work in front of slipped st. Do not position beads on edge stitches of work as this will interfere with seaming.
dec2 = slip next 2 sts as though to K2tog, then K1, pass 2 slipped sts over.

BACK AND FRONT (BOTH ALIKE)

Outer hem edging
Using size 8 (5mm) needles and waste yarn, cast on 14 sts.

Beg with a K row, work in St st for 4 rows, ending with RS facing for next row. Break off waste yarn and join in yarn MC. Cont in border patt as foll:
Row 1 (RS): Sl 1, K2tog, yo, K1, yo, K2tog tbl, (K1, yo) twice, (K1, yo, K1) into next st, (yo, K1) twice, (yo) twice, K2tog, K1. 21 sts.
Row 2: K2, (K1, P1) into double yo of previous row, K1, P9, K1, P5, K1.
Row 3: Sl 1, K2tog, yo, K1, yo, K2tog tbl, K1, (yo, K3) 3 times, yo, K1, (yo) twice, K1, (yo) twice, K2tog, K1. 28 sts.
Row 4: K2, (K1, P1) into double yo of previous row, K1, (K1, P1) into double yo of previous row, K1, P5, P3tog, (P5, K1) twice. 26 sts.
Row 5: Sl 1, K2tog, yo, K1, yo, K2tog tbl, K1, (yo, K2tog tbl, K1, K2tog, yo, K1) twice, *(yo) twice, K2tog, rep from * twice more, K1. 29 sts.
Row 6: K2, *(K1, P1) into double yo of previous row, K1, rep from * twice more, P2tog, P1, P2tog tbl, P1, P2tog, P1, P2tog tbl, K1, P5, K1. 25 sts.
Row 7: Sl 1, K2tog, yo, K1, yo, K2tog tbl, K1, yo, sl 2 as though to K2tog, K1, p2sso, K1, sl 2 as though to K2tog, K1, p2sso, yo, K11. 23 sts.
Row 8: Bind off 7 sts, K until there are 5 sts on right needle, P3tog, K2, P5, K1. 14 sts.
These 8 rows form border patt.
Cont in border patt until edging measures 20¹/₂ [21¹/₂, 22¹/₂, 23¹/₂, 24¹/₂] in./52 [55, 57, 60, 62]cm from first row in yarn MC, ending after patt row 8 and with RS facing for next row.
Break off yarn MC and join in waste yarn. Beg with a K row, work in St st for 4 rows, ending with RS facing for next row. Bind off.

Inner hem edging
Work as for outer hem edging but using

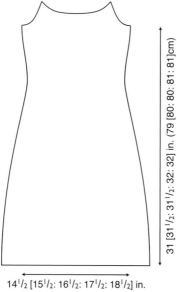

31 [31¹/₂: 31¹/₂: 32: 32] in. (79 [80: 80: 81: 81]cm)

14¹/₂ [15¹/₂: 16¹/₂: 17¹/₂: 18¹/₂] in.
(37 [39.5: 42: 44: 46.5]cm)

Lace Blouse

This is a must-have cotton knit. The V-neck and cap sleeves are very flattering for all figure shapes. You can wear it any time, any place. It goes beautifully with the Cotton Camisole on page 12 and a summer skirt. It is ideal, too, to wear under a winter suit for the office, and then without the jacket in the evening.

LACE BLOUSE by Jennie Atkinson

SIZES

	XS	S	M	L	XL	
To fit bust	32	34	36	38	40	in.
	81	86	91	97	102	cm

For actual size, see diagram below.

YARN

5 [5, 6, 6, 7] balls of Rowan *4-Ply Cotton* (50g/1¾oz) in desired shade (Bleached 113 was used here)

NEEDLES

Pair each of size 2 (3mm) and size 3 (3.25mm) knitting needles

EXTRAS

7 buttons

GAUGE

22 sts and 38 rows to 4 in./10cm measured over pattern using size 3 (3.25mm) needles.

BACK

Using size 2 (3.25mm) needles, cast on 92 [98, 104, 110, 116] sts.

Work 25 [27, 29, 31, 33] rows in garter st (knit every row).

Beg lace patt as foll:

Row 1 (RS): K1, *yo, K1, rep from * to last st, K1.

Row 2: K1, P to last st, K1.

Row 3: K1, *K2tog, rep from * to last st, K1.

Row 4: K1, *yo, K2tog, rep from * to last st, K1.

Row 5: Rep row 4.

Rows 6 and 7: K to end.

These 7 rows form patt and are repeated throughout. (**Note:** Every other 7-row patt repeat starts with row 1 as a WS row.)

Work 21 more rows in patt.

Change to size 3 (3.25mm) needles.

Cont in patt until back measures 11 [11½, 11¾, 12¼, 12½] in./28 [29, 30, 31, 32]cm from cast-on edge, ending with RS facing for next row.

Sleeve shaping

Keeping patt correct as set throughout, cast on 4 sts at beg of next 6 [8, 10, 12, 14] rows. 116 [130, 144, 158, 172] sts.

Work even until back measures 18 [19, 19¾, 20½, 21¼] in./46 [48, 50, 52, 54]cm from cast-on edge, ending with RS facing for next row.

Shape shoulders and upper sleeves

Bind off 6 sts at beg of next 12 [14, 16, 18, 20] rows.

Bind off rem 44 [46, 48, 50, 52] sts.

LEFT FRONT

Using size 2 (3mm) needles, cast on 30 [34, 38, 42, 46] sts.

Work 25 [27, 29, 31, 33] rows in garter st.

Work 28 rows in patt as given for back.

Change to size 3 (3.25mm) needles.

Cont in patt until front measures 11 [11½, 11¾, 12¼, 12½] in./28 [29, 30, 31, 32]cm from cast-on edge, ending with RS facing for next row.

Sleeve shaping

Keeping patt correct as set throughout, cast on 4 sts at beg of the next row and EOR 2 [3, 4, 5, 6] times. 42 [50, 58, 66, 74] sts.

Work even for 9 [7, 5, 3, 1] rows.

Shape neck

Dec one st at neck edge of next row and every 10th [8th, 6th, 6th, 4th] row 5 [7, 9, 11, 13] times. 36 [42, 48, 54, 60] sts.

Work even until front measures same as back to shoulder shaping, ending at armhole edge.

Shape shoulder and upper sleeve

Bind off 6 sts at beg of next row and EOR 4 [5, 6, 7, 8] times.

Work even for 1 row.

Bind off rem 6 sts.

RIGHT FRONT

Using size 2 (3mm) needles, cast on 30 [34, 38, 42, 46] sts.

Work 25 [27, 29, 31, 33] rows in garter st.

Work 28 rows in patt as given for back.

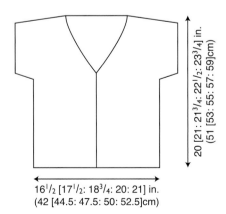

20 [21: 21¾: 22½: 23¾] in.
(51 [53: 55: 57: 59]cm)

16½ [17½: 18¾: 20: 21] in.
(42 [44.5: 47.5: 50: 52.5]cm)

Change to size 3 (3.25mm) needles.
Cont in patt until front measures 11
[11½, 11¾, 12¼, 12½] in./28 [29, 30, 31,
32]cm from cast-on edge, ending with **WS**
facing for next row.

Sleeve shaping

Keeping patt correct as set throughout,
cast on 4 sts at beg of next row and
2 [3, 4, 5, 6] foll alt rows. 42 [50, 58, 66,
74] sts.

Work even for 8 [6, 4, 2, 0] rows.

Shape neck

Dec one st at neck edge of next row and
every 10th [8th, 6th, 6th, 4th] row 5 [7, 9,
11, 13] times. 36 [42, 48, 54, 60] sts.

Work even until front measures same as
back to shoulder shaping, ending at
armhole edge.

Shape shoulder and upper sleeve seam

Bind off 6 sts at beg of next and 4 [5, 6, 7,
8] foll alt rows.

Work even for 1 row.

Bind off rem 6 sts.

FINISHING

Block then press lightly on WS, following
instructions on yarn label.

Sew shoulder and upper sleeve seams.

Sew side and under sleeve seams.

Border

Using size 2 (3mm) needles, cast on
17 sts.

Knit 1 row.

Work in patt as foll:

Row 1 (RS): K4, (yo, K1, K2tog) twice, yo,
K3, yo, K4. 19 sts.

Row 2: K4, yo, K5, (yo, P2tog, K1) twice,
yo, K4. 21 sts.

Row 3: K4, (yo, K1, K2tog) twice, yo, K1,
yo, skp, K1, K2tog, yo, K1, yo, K4. 23 sts.

Row 4: K4, yo, K3, yo, P3tog, yo, K3, (yo,
P2tog, K1) twice, yo, K4. 25 sts.

Row 5: K5, K2tog, yo, K1, K2tog, yo, K11,
yo, K4. 26 sts.

Row 6: K2tog, K3, yo, P2tog, K1, P2tog tbl,
yo, K1, yo, P2tog, K1, P2tog tbl, (yo, K1,
P2tog) twice, K4. 24 sts.

Row 7: K4, (yo, skp, K1) twice, yo, sl 1,
K2tog, psso, yo, K3, yo, K3tog, yo, K3,
K2tog. 23 sts.

Row 8: K2tog, K3, yo, P2tog, K3, P2tog tbl,
(yo, K1, P2tog tbl) twice, yo, K2tog, K3.
21 sts.

Row 9: K3, K2tog, yo, skp, (K1, yo, skp)
twice, K1, K2tog, yo, K3, K2tog. 19 sts.

Row 10: K2tog, K3, yo, P3tog, (yo, K1,
P2tog tbl) twice, yo, K2tog, K3. 17 sts.

Row 11: K3, K2tog, yo, skp, K1, yo, skp, K2,
yo, K3, K2tog. 16 sts.

Row 12: K2tog, K3, yo, K1, (yo, P2tog, K1)
twice, yo, K4. 17 sts.

These 12 rows form patt and are repeated
throughout.

Cont in patt until border fits up left front,
around back neck and down right front.
Bind off.

Sew border in place.

Sew buttons to left front border, the first
to come ½ in./1.5cm from lower edge,
the last ³⁄₈ in./1cm below front neck
shaping, and the other five equally spaced
between. Use eyelets in right front lace
border as buttonholes.

Beaded Jacket

This little cotton jacket is wonderfully easy to wear and transforms from daywear to an evening out just by the way you accessorize it, as with a wide satin-ribbon tie around the waist shown here. The beads make it dressy enough for an evening cover-up, but the jacket style is crisp enough for daywear, too. The slightly flared peplum in seed stitch flatters most people, as does the neat, small collar.

BEADED JACKET by Kim Hargreaves

SIZES

	XS	S	M	L	XL	
To fit bust	32	34	36	38	40	in.
	81	86	91	97	102	cm

For actual size, see diagram below.

YARN

10 [11, 12, 12, 13] balls of Rowan *Cotton Glace* (50g/1³/₄oz) in desired shade (Ecru 725 was used here)

NEEDLES

Pair each of size 2 (3mm) and size 3 (3.25mm) knitting needles

EXTRAS

11mm abalone or mother-of-pearl buttons, 8 (Rowan no. 00322 Abalone) 3mm round glass beads, approximately 660 [710, 760, 790, 800], in pink (Rowan no. 01015)

GAUGE

23 sts and 39 rows to 4 in./10cm measured over seed st using size 3 (3.25mm) needles.
23 sts and 32 rows to 4 in./10cm measured over stockinette stitch using size 3 (3.25mm) needles.

SPECIAL ABBREVIATIONS

b1 (bead 1) = bring yarn to RS of work, slide bead up next to stitch just worked, slip next stitch purlwise from left needle to right needle and take yarn back to WS of work, leaving bead sitting on RS of work in front of slipped st. Do not position beads on edge stitches of work as this will interfere with seaming.

PATTERN NOTE

Number of beads given for back, fronts, and sleeves are estimates; total amount of beads specified for each size is generous, so more beads can be added if necessary. Thread beads onto yarn as explained on page 124.

BACK

Lower section

Using size 2 (3mm) needles, cast on 99 [105, 111, 117, 123] sts.
Row 1 (RS): K1, *P1, K1, rep from * to end.
Row 2: Rep row 1.
These 2 rows form seed st.
Work in 4 more rows in seed st, ending with RS facing for next row.
Change to size 3 (3.25mm) needles.
Work 14 more rows in seed st, ending with a RS facing for next row.
Place markers on 26th [28th, 30th, 32nd, 34th] st in from both ends of last row.
Next row (dec row) (RS): Work 2tog, seed st to within one st of first marker, work 3tog (marked st is center st of this group), seed st to within one st of 2nd marker, work 3tog (marked st is center st of this group), seed st to last 2 sts, work 2tog.
Work even in seed st for 15 rows.
Rep last 16 rows once more, then first of these rows (the dec row) again.
81 [87, 93, 99, 105] sts.
Work even in seed st for 9 rows, ending with a RS facing for next row.
Bind off in seed st.

Upper section

Thread 150 [170, 190, 200, 210] beads onto yarn. Then with WS facing (so that ridge is formed on RS of work) and using size 3 (3.25mm) needles, pick up and knit 81 [87, 93, 99, 105] sts across bound-off edge of lower section.
Beg with a K row, work in St st for 8 rows, ending with RS facing for next row.
Cont in patt as foll:
Row 1 (RS): K2, M1, K6 [1, 4, 7, 2], *b1, K7, rep from * to last 9 [4, 7, 10, 5] sts, b1, K6 [1, 4, 7, 2], M1, K2.
Working all side seam increases as set by last row and beg with a P row, work in St st for 9 rows, inc one st at each end of 6th of these rows.
85 [91, 97, 103, 109] sts.
Row 11 (RS): K6 [9, 4, 7, 2], *b1, K7, rep from * to last 7 [10, 5, 8, 3] sts, b1, K6 [9, 4, 7, 2].
Beg with a P row, work in St st for 9 rows, inc one st at each end of 2nd and foll 6th row. 89 [95, 101, 107, 113] sts.
Last 20 rows form patt and start side seam shaping.
Cont in patt, shaping side seams by inc one st at each end of 5th row and every

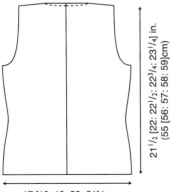

17 [18: 19: 20: 21] in.
(43 [45.5: 48.5: 51: 53.5]cm)

21¹/₂ [22: 22¹/₂: 22³/₄: 23¹/₄] in.
(55 [56: 57: 58: 59]cm)

14¹/₄ [14¹/₄: 14¹/₂: 14¹/₂: 14¹/₂] in.
(36 [36: 37: 37: 37]cm)

foll 6th row until there are 95 [101, 107, 113, 119] sts, then on every foll 4th row until there are 99 [105, 111, 117, 123] sts, taking inc sts into patt.

Work even until back measures 13¾ [14¼, 14¼, 14½, 14½] in./35 [36, 36, 37, 37]cm *from cast-on edge of lower section*, ending with RS facing for next row.

Shape armholes

Keeping patt correct, bind off 3 [4, 4, 5, 5] sts at beg of next 2 rows.
93 [97, 103, 107, 113] sts.

Dec one st at each end of next 5 [5, 7, 7, 9] rows, then EOR 2 [3, 3, 4, 4] times, then on foll 4th row.
77 [79, 81, 83, 85] sts.

Work even until armhole measures 7¾ [7¾, 8¼, 8¼, 8¾] in./20 [20, 21, 21, 22]cm, ending with RS facing for next row.

Shape shoulders and back neck

Bind off 8 sts at beg of next 2 rows.
61 [63, 65, 67, 69] sts.

Next row (RS): Bind off 8 sts, patt until there are 11 [11, 12, 12, 13] sts on right needle, then turn, leaving rem sts on a holder.

Work each side of neck separately.
Bind off 4 sts at beg of next row.
Bind off rem 7 [7, 8, 8, 9] sts.

With RS facing, rejoin yarn to rem sts, bind off center 23 [25, 25, 27, 27] sts, patt to end.

Complete to match first side, reversing shapings.

LEFT FRONT

Lower section

Using size 2 (3mm) needles, cast on 53 [56, 59, 62, 65] sts.

Row 1 (RS): *K1, P1, rep from * to last 1 [0, 1, 0, 1] st, K1 [0, 1, 0, 1].

Row 2: K1 [0, 1, 0, 1], *P1, K1, rep from * to end.

These 2 rows form seed st.

Work 4 more rows in seed st, ending with RS facing for next row.

Change to size 3 (3.25mm) needles.

Work 14 more rows in seed st, ending with RS facing for next row.

Place marker on 26th [28th, 30th, 32nd, 34th] st in from end of last row.

Next row (dec row) (RS): Work 2tog, seed st to within one st of marker, work 3tog (marked st is center st of this group), seed st to end.

Work 15 rows in seed st.

Rep last 16 rows once more, then first of these rows (the dec row) again.
44 [47, 50, 53, 56] sts.

Work 9 more rows in seed st, ending with RS facing for next row.

Next row (RS): Bind off first 39 [42, 45, 48, 51] sts, seed st to end.

Break off yarn and thread 75 [90, 95, 100, 105] beads onto yarn.

Upper section

Using size 3 (3.25mm) needles, rejoin yarn and seed st 5 sts on needle, then with WS facing (so that ridge is formed on RS of work), pick up and knit 39 [42, 45, 48, 51] sts across bound-off edge of lower section. 44 [47, 50, 53, 56] sts.

Next row (RS): K to last 5 sts, seed st 5 sts.

Next row: Seed st 5 sts, P to end.

These 2 rows set the sts (front opening edge 5 sts still in seed st with all other sts in St st).

Work 6 more rows as set, ending with RS facing for next row.

Cont in patt as foll:

Row 1 (RS): K2, M1, K6 [1, 4, 7, 2], *b1, K7, rep from * to last 12 sts, b1, K6, seed st 5 sts.

Working all side seam increases as set by last row, keeping seed st border correct and working all other sts in St st, beg with a P row, work 9 rows, inc one st at beg of 6th of these rows. 46 [49, 52, 55, 58] sts.

Row 11 (RS): K6 [9, 4, 7, 2], *b1, K7, rep from * to last 8 sts, b1, K2, seed st 5 sts.

Work 9 rows, inc one st at beg of 2nd and foll 6th row. 48 [51, 54, 57, 60] sts.

Last 20 rows form patt and start side seam shaping.

Cont in patt, shaping side seam by inc one st at beg of 5th row and every foll 6th row to 51 [54, 57, 60, 63] sts, then on every foll 4th row until there are 53 [56, 59, 62, 65] sts, taking inc sts into patt.

Work even until left front matches back to beg of armhole shaping, ending with RS facing for next row.

Shape armhole

Keeping patt correct, bind off 3 [4, 4, 5, 5] sts at beg of next row.
50 [52, 55, 57, 60] sts.

Work 1 row.

Dec one st at armhole edge of next 5 [5, 7, 7, 9] rows, then EOR 2 [3, 3, 4, 4] times, then on foll 4th row.
42 [43, 44, 45, 46] sts.

Work even until 22 [22, 22, 24, 24] fewer rows have been worked to start of shoulder shaping than on back, ending with RS facing for next row.

Shape lapel

Next row (RS): Patt to last 5 sts, seed st 5 sts.

Next row: Seed st 6 sts, P to end.

Next row: Patt to last 7 sts, seed st 7 sts.

Next row: Seed st 8 sts, P to end.

Work 8 [9, 9, 10, 10] rows, working one extra st in seed on every row as set by last 4 rows (16 [17, 17, 18, 18] sts now in seed st).

Work 10 [9, 9, 10, 10] more rows but now working one extra st in seed st on 3rd and every foll 3rd row, ending with RS facing for next row (19 [20, 20, 21, 21] sts now in seed st).

Shape shoulder

Bind off 8 sts at beg of next row and foll

alt row, then 7 [7, 8, 8, 9] sts at beg of foll alt row.

Work 1 row, ending with RS facing for next row.

Break off yarn and leave rem 19 [20, 20, 21, 21] sts on a holder.

Mark positions for 7 buttons along opening edge of upper section, first to come in row 5, last to come 6 rows below lapel shaping and rem 5 buttons evenly spaced between.

RIGHT FRONT

Lower section

Using size 2 (3mm) needles, cast on 53 [56, 59, 62, 65] sts.

Row 1 (RS): K1 [0, 1, 0, 1], *P1, K1, rep from * to end.

Row 2: *K1, P1, rep from * to last 1 [0, 1, 0, 1] st, K1 [0, 1, 0, 1].

These 2 rows form seed st.

Work 4 more rows in seed st, ending with RS facing for next row.

Change to size 3 (3.25mm) needles.

Work 14 more rows in seed st, ending with RS facing for next row.

Place marker on 26th [28th, 30th, 32nd, 34th] st in from beg of last row.

Next row (dec row) (RS): Seed st to within one st of marker, work 3tog (marked st is center st of this group), seed st to last 2 sts, work 2tog.

Work 15 rows in seed st.

Rep last 16 rows once more, then first of these rows (the dec row) again.
44 [47, 50, 53, 56] sts.

Work 3 more rows in seed st, ending with RS facing for next row.

Next row (RS): Seed st 2 sts, work 2tog, yo (to make first buttonhole), seed st to end.

Work 5 more rows in seed st, ending with RS facing for next row.

Next row (RS): Seed st 5 sts, bind off

rem 39 [42, 45, 48, 51] sts.

Break off yarn and thread 75 [90, 95, 100, 105] beads onto yarn.

Upper section

With WS facing (so that ridge is formed on RS of work) and using size 3 (3.25mm) needles, rejoin yarn and pick up and knit 39 [42, 45, 48, 51] sts across bound-off edge of lower section, then seed st rem 5 sts. 44 [47, 50, 53, 56] sts.

Next row (RS): Seed st 5 sts, K to end.

Next row: P to last 5 sts, seed st 5 sts.

These 2 rows set the sts (front opening edge 5 sts still in seed st with all other sts in St st).

Work 2 more rows as set, ending with RS facing for next row.

Next row (RS): Seed st 2 sts, work 2tog, yo (to make a buttonhole), patt to end.

Working 6 buttonholes more in this way to correspond with positions marked for buttons on left front and noting that no more reference will be made to buttonholes, cont as foll:

Work 3 more rows as set, ending with RS facing for next row.

Cont in patt as foll:

Row 1 (RS): Seed st 5 sts, K6, *b1, K7, rep from * to last 9 [4, 7, 10, 5] sts, b1, K6 [1, 4, 7, 2], M1, K2.

Working all side seam increases as set by last row, keeping seed st border correct and working all other sts in St st, beg with a P row, work 9 rows, inc one st at end of 6th of these rows.
46 [49, 52, 55, 58] sts.

Row 11 (RS): Seed st 5 sts, K2, *b1, K7, rep from * to last 7 [10, 5, 8, 3] sts, b1, K6 [9, 4, 7, 2].

Work 9 rows, inc one st at end of 2nd row and foll 6th row.
48 [51, 54, 57, 60] sts.

Last 20 rows form patt and start side seam shaping.

Cont in patt, shaping side seam by inc one st at end of 5th row and every foll 6th row to 51 [54, 57, 60, 63] sts, then on every foll 4th row until there are 53 [56, 59, 62, 65] sts, taking inc sts into patt.

Work even until right front matches back to beg of armhole shaping, ending with *WS* facing for next row.

Shape armhole

Keeping patt correct, bind off 3 [4, 4, 5, 5] sts at beg of next row.
50 [52, 55, 57, 60] sts.

Dec one st at armhole edge of next 5 [5, 7, 7, 9] rows, then EOR 2 [3, 3, 4, 4] times, then on foll 4th row.
42 [43, 44, 45, 46] sts.

Work even until 22 [22, 22, 24, 24] fewer rows have been worked to start of shoulder shaping than on back, ending with RS facing for next row.

Shape lapel

Next row (RS): Seed st 5 sts, patt to end.

Next row: Patt to last 6 sts, seed st 6 sts.

Next row: Seed st 7 sts, patt to end.

Next row: Patt to last 8 sts, seed st 8 sts.

Work 8 [9, 9, 10, 10] rows, working one extra st in seed on every row as set by last 4 rows (16 [17, 17, 18, 18] sts now in seed st).

Work 11 [10, 10, 11, 11] more rows but now working one extra st in seed st on 3rd row and every foll 3rd row, ending with a RS row (19 [20, 20, 21, 21] sts now in seed st).

Shape shoulder

Bind off 8 sts at beg of next and foll alt row, then 7 [7, 8, 8, 9] sts at beg of foll alt row, ending with RS facing for next row.

Do NOT break yarn but leave rem 19 [20, 20, 21, 21] sts on a holder and set aside this ball of yarn.

SLEEVES (BOTH ALIKE)

Thread half of rem beads onto yarn.

Using size 3 (3.25mm) needles, cast on 59 [59, 61, 63, 63] sts.

Beg with a K row, work in St st for 10 rows, ending with RS facing for next row.

Cont in patt as foll:

Row 1 (RS): K5 [5, 6, 7, 7], *b1, K7, rep from * to last 6 [6, 7, 8, 8] sts, b1, K5 [5, 6, 7, 7].

Working all inc in same way as for back and fronts and beg with a P row, work in St st for 9 rows, inc one st at each end of 4th of these rows.

61 [61, 63, 65, 65] sts.

Row 11 (RS): K2 [2, 3, 4, 4], *b1, K7, rep from * to last 3 [3, 4, 5, 5] sts, b1, K2 [2, 3, 4, 4].

Beg with a P row, work in St st for 9 rows, inc one st at each end of 0 [8th, 8th, 8th, 6th] of these rows. 61 [63, 65, 67, 67] sts.

Last 20 rows form patt and start sleeve shaping.

Cont in patt, shaping sides by inc one st at each end of next [11th, 13th, 13th, 9th] row and every foll 14th [12th, 12th, 12th, 12th] row until there are 73 [75, 77, 79, 73] sts, then *for largest size only* on every foll 10th row until there are 81 sts, taking inc sts into patt.

Work even until sleeve measures 14¼ [14¼, 14½, 14½, 14½] in./36 [36, 37, 37, 37]cm from cast-on edge, ending with RS facing for next row.

Shape sleeve cap

Keeping patt correct, bind off 3 [4, 4, 5, 5] sts at beg of next 2 rows.

67 [67, 69, 69, 71] sts.

Dec one st at each end of next 5 rows, then on foll 2 alt rows, then on every foll 4th row until 41 [41, 43, 43, 45] sts rem.

Work 1 row, ending with RS facing for next row.

Dec one st at each end of next row and

every foll alt row until 35 sts rem, then on foll row, ending with RS facing for next row. 33 sts.

Bind off 4 sts at beg of next 2 rows.

Bind off rem 25 sts.

FINISHING

Block then press lightly on WS, following instructions on yarn label and avoiding seed st.

Sew both shoulder seams using backstitch.

Collar

With RS facing and using size 2 (3mm) needles and ball of yarn set to one side with right front, seed st across 19 [20, 20, 21, 21] sts of right front, pick up and knit 31 [33, 33, 35, 35] sts from back, then seed st across 19 [20, 20, 21, 21] sts of

left front. 69 [73, 73, 77, 77] sts.

Work in seed st as set by fronts for 1¼ in./3cm.

Bind off in seed st.

Cuffs (both alike)

Using size 2 (3mm) needles, cast on 63 [63, 65, 67, 67] sts.

Work in seed st as given for back for 3 in./7.5cm. Bind off in seed st.

Sew side seams. Sew sleeve seams and set in sleeves as explained on page 124.

Sew together row-end edges of cuffs for 1¼ in./3cm from bound-off edge.

Aligning cuff seam with sleeve seam, sew bound-off edge of each cuff to lower edge of sleeve. Fold cuffs to RS.

Sew on buttons to correspond with buttonholes.

Beaded Shrug

Another gossamer-like design, this could be the perfect partner for the Butterfly Dress on page 23 if knitted in the same or a matching color. It is delicately beaded around the front and the edge of the hood to add a little bit of evening sparkle. The beads are added with very sim crochet stitches, so all you need are the basic crochet skills. If you prefer a try the one on page 70.

BEADED SHRUG by Jennie Atkinson

SIZES

	XS–S	M–L	
To fit bust	32–34	36–38	in.
	81–86	91–97	cm

For actual size, see diagram below.

YARN

5 [6] balls of Rowan *Kidsilk Haze* (25g/1oz) in main color **MC** and one ball in contrasting color **CC** (Drab 588 was used here for MC and Majestic 589 for CC)

NEEDLES AND HOOK

Pair each of size 5 (3.75mm) and size 8 (5mm) knitting needles
Size E-4 (3.50mm) crochet hook

EXTRAS

3mm round glass beads, 118 each in gold and copper (Rowan nos. 01006 and 01009)

GAUGE

26 sts and 24 rows to 4 in./10cm measured

with a rib row 2.
Change to size 8 (5mm) needles and beg patt as foll:
Patt row 1 (RS): P to end.
Patt row 2: K1,*(K1, P1, K1) all in next st, P3tog, rep from * to last st, K1.
Patt row 3: P to end.
Patt row 4: K1, *P3tog, (K1, P1, K1) all in next st, rep from * to last st, K1.
These 4 rows form patt and are repeated throughout.
Work even in patt until sleeve measures 16½ in./42cm from cast-on edge, ending with RS facing for next row. Mark each end of last row with a colored thread.

Right front shaping
Keeping patt correct as set throughout, bind off 4 sts at beg of next row and EOR 14 [15] times. 74 [78] sts.
Work even for 1 row; mark end of this row with a colored thread.
Bind off 8 sts at beg of next row.
66 [70] sts.
Work 2¾ [4 ¾] in./7 [12]cm more, ending

ext row; mark
lored thread.

ext row and EOR
sts.
w with a colored

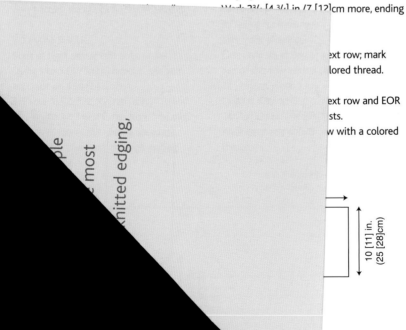

10 [11] in.
(25 [28]cm)

Work even until sleeve measures 14 in./36cm from colored threads, ending with RS facing for next row.
Change to size 5 (3.75mm) needles.
Rib row 1: K2, *P2, K2, rep from * to end.
Rib row 2: P2, *K2, P2, rep from * to end.
Rep last 2 rows until ribbing measures 2½ in./6cm, ending with a rib row 2.
Bind off in rib.

HOOD

Using size 8 (5mm) needles and yarn MC, cast on 86 [98] sts.
Work even in patt as for shrug until hood measures 13 in./33cm from cast-on edge, ending with RS facing for next row.
Bind off.

FINISHING

Fold hood in half and sew bound-off edges together. Sew cast-on edge of hood to neck edge between markers, easing in fullness. Sew sleeve seams.
Main edging
Alternating two colors, thread 236 beads onto yarn.
With **WS** facing and using size E-4 (3.50mm) hook and yarn CC, join yarn to lower edge of shrug at center back.
Round 1 (WS): Ch1, work sc evenly around edge, working 35sc to underarm seam, 52sc to beg of neck, 180sc around front edge of hood, 52sc to underarm seam, 36sc to center back, join with a slip st in first sc. 355sc. Do not turn at end of rounds, but work with **WS** always facing.
Round 2: *Skip 2sc, 1dc in next sc, (slide bead up to hook, 1dc in same sc as last dc was worked) 4 times, skip 2sc, 1 slip st in next sc, rep from * to end of round, working last slip st in slip st at beg of round. (Note that beads worked in way described will sit on RS of shrug.)
Fasten off.

Chevron Lace Top

This 30s revival design with its white-trimmed collar and figure-hugging shape is really versatile. Airy enough for summer, it makes a good autumn standby to wear with a suit, too. Dress it down with cotton pants in summer, or dress it up with a smart tweed skirt in winter. Knitted in Rowan's 4-Ply Cotton, the lacy pattern is stretchy and very comfortable to wear.

CHEVRON LACE TOP by Kim Hargreaves

SIZES

	XS	S	M	L	XL	
To fit bust	32	34	36	38	40	in.
	81	86	91	97	102	cm

For actual size, see diagram below.

YARN

8 [9, 9, 10, 10] balls of Rowan *4-Ply Cotton* (50g/1¾oz) in main color **MC** and one ball in contrasting color **CC** (Ripple 121 was used here for MC and Bleached 113 for CC)

NEEDLES

Pair each of size 1 (2.25mm) and size 2 (3mm) knitting needles

EXTRAS

11mm abalone or mother-of-pearl buttons, 5 (Rowan no. 00322)

GAUGE

28 sts and 40 rows to 4 in./10cm measured over pattern using size 2 (3mm) needles.

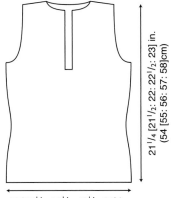

16 [17½: 18½: 19½: 21] in.
(41 [44: 47: 49.5: 52.5]cm)

21¼ [21½: 22: 22½: 23] in.
(54 [55: 56: 57: 58]cm)

BACK

Using size 1 (2.25mm) needles and yarn CC, cast on 115 [123, 131, 139, 147] sts. Break off yarn CC and join in yarn MC.
Row 1 (RS): K1, *P1, K1, rep from * to end.
Row 2: P1, *K1, P1, rep from * to end.
Last 2 rows form rib.
Cont in rib, dec one st at each end of 13th and every foll 6th row until 103 [111, 119, 127, 135] sts rem.
Work 3 more rows in rib, ending with RS facing for next row.
Change to size 2 (3mm) needles.
Row 1 (RS): K4, place marker, *K2tog tbl, (K1, yo) twice, K1, K2tog, K1, rep from * to last 3 sts, place marker, K3. (Slip markers on foll rows.)
Row 2: P3, *P1, P2tog, (P1, yo) twice, P1, P2tog tbl, rep from * to last 4 sts, P4.
Row 3: K2tog, K2, *yo, K2tog tbl, K3, K2tog, yo, K1, rep from * to last 3 sts, K1, K2tog. 101 [109, 117, 125, 133] sts.
Row 4: P2, *P2, yo, P2tog, P1, P2tog tbl, yo, P1, rep from * to last 3 sts, P3.

Row 5: K3, *K2, yo, sl 1, K2tog, psso, yo, K3; rep from * to last 2 sts, K2.
Row 6: P2, *P1, P2tog, (P1, yo) twice, P1, P2tog tbl, rep from * to last 3 sts, P3.
Row 7: K3, *K2tog tbl, (K1, yo) twice, K1, K2tog, K1, rep from * to last 2 sts, K2.
Row 8: P2, *P1, yo, P2tog, P3, P2tog tbl, yo, rep from * to last 3 sts, P3.
Row 9: K2tog, K1, *K1, yo, K2tog tbl, K1, K2tog, yo, K2, rep from * to last 2 sts, K2tog. 99 [107, 115, 123, 131] sts.
Row 10: P1, *P3, yo, P3tog, yo, P2, rep from * to last 2 sts, P2.
These 10 rows form patt and cont side seam shaping. (**Note:** When working patt, cont to work edge sts outside markers in St st and sts inside markers following the 8-st patt repeat.)
Cont in patt, shaping side seams by inc one st at each end of 11th row and every foll 10th row until there are 107 [115, 123, 131, 139] sts, then on every foll 8th row until there are 115 [123, 131, 139, 147] sts, taking inc sts into St st until there are sufficient to take into patt.
Work even until back measures 14¼ [14½, 14½, 15, 15] in./36 [37, 37, 38, 38]cm, ending with RS facing for next row.
Shape armholes
Keeping patt correct throughout, bind off 5 [6, 6, 7, 7] sts at beg of next 2 rows. 105 [111, 119, 125, 133] sts.
Dec one st at each end of next 5 [5, 7, 7, 9] rows, then on EOR 3 [5, 5, 7, 7] times. 89 [91, 95, 97, 101] sts.
Work even until armhole measures 7 [7, 7½, 7½, 8] in./18 [18, 19, 19, 20]cm, ending with RS facing for next row.
Shape shoulders and back neck
Bind off 8 [8, 9, 9, 10] sts at beg of next 2 rows. 73 [75, 77, 79, 81] sts.
Next row (RS): Bind off 8 [8, 9, 9, 10] sts, patt until there are 13 sts on right

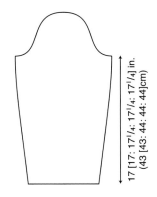

17 [17: 17¼: 17¼: 17¼] in.
(43 [43: 44: 44: 44]cm)

needle, then turn, leaving rem sts on a holder.

Work each side of neck separately.

Bind off 4 sts at beg of next row.

Bind off rem 9 sts.

With RS facing, rejoin yarn to rem sts, bind off center 31 [33, 33, 35, 35] sts, patt to end.

Complete to match first side, reversing shapings.

FRONT

Work as given for back until 8 fewer rows have been worked than on back to beg of armhole shaping, ending with RS facing for next row.

Divide for front opening

Next row (RS): Patt 54 [58, 62, 66, 70] sts, then turn, leaving rem sts on a holder.

Work each side of neck separately.

Work 7 rows, ending with RS facing for next row.

Shape armhole

Keeping patt correct throughout, bind off 5 [6, 6, 7, 7] sts at beg of next row. 49 [52, 56, 59, 63] sts.

Work 1 row.

Dec one st at armhole edge of next 5 [5, 7, 7, 9] rows, then on EOR 3 [5, 5, 7, 7] times. 41 [42, 44, 45, 47] sts.

Work even until 23 [23, 23, 25, 25] fewer rows have been worked than on back to start of shoulder shaping, ending with WS facing for next row.

Shape neck

Keeping patt correct, bind off 6 [7, 7, 7, 7] sts at beg of next row. 35 [35, 37, 38, 40] sts.

Dec one st at neck edge of next 5 rows, then on EOR 4 [4, 4, 5, 5] times, then on foll 4th row. 25 [25, 27, 27, 29] sts.

Work 5 rows, ending with RS facing for next row.

Shape shoulder

Bind off 8 [8, 9, 9, 10] sts at beg of next and foll alt row.

Work 1 row.

Bind off rem 9 sts.

With RS facing, rejoin yarn to rem sts, bind off center 7 sts, patt to end.

Complete to match first side, reversing shapings.

SLEEVES (BOTH ALIKE)

Using size 1 (2.25mm) needles and yarn CC, cast on 63 [63, 65, 67, 67] sts.

Break off yarn CC and join in yarn MC.

Work in rib as given for back, shaping sides by inc one st at each end of 15th and foll 12th [10th, 10th, 10th, 10th] row, taking inc sts into rib.

67 [67, 69, 71, 71] sts.

Work 5 [7, 7, 7, 7] more rows in rib, ending with RS facing for next row.

Change to size 2 (3mm) needles.

Row 1 (RS): K2 [2, 3, 4, 4], place marker, *K2tog tbl, (K1, yo) twice, K1, K2tog, K1, rep from * to last 1 [1, 2, 3, 3] sts, place marker, K1 [1, 2, 3, 3]. (Slip markers on foll rows.)

Row 2: P1 [1, 2, 3, 3], *P1, P2tog, (P1, yo) twice, P1, P2tog tbl, rep from * to last 2 [2, 3, 4, 4] sts, P2 [2, 3, 4, 4].

Row 3: (Inc in first st) 0 [1, 1, 1, 1] times, K2 [1, 2, 3, 3], *yo, K2tog tbl, K3, K2tog, yo, K1, rep from * to last 1 [1, 2, 3, 3] sts, K1 [0, 1, 2, 2], (inc in last st) 0 [1, 1, 1, 1] times. 67 [69, 71, 73, 73] sts.

Row 4: P1 [2, 3, 4, 4], *P2, yo, P2tog, P1, P2tog tbl, yo, P1, rep from * to last 2 [3, 4, 5, 5] sts, P2 [3, 4, 5, 5].

Row 5: (Inc in first st) 1 [0, 0, 0, 0] times, K1 [3, 4, 5, 5], *K2, yo, sl 1, K2tog, psso, yo, K3; rep from * to last 1 [2, 3, 4, 4] sts, K0 [2, 3, 4, 4], (inc in last st) 1 [0, 0, 0, 0] times. 69 [69, 71, 73, 73] sts.

Row 6: P2 [2, 3, 4, 4], *P1, P2tog, (P1, yo) twice, P1, P2tog tbl, rep from * to last 3 [3, 4, 5, 5] sts, P3 [3, 4, 5, 5].

Row 7: K3 [3, 4, 5, 5], *K2tog tbl, (K1, yo) twice, K1, K2tog, K1, rep from * to last 2 [2, 3, 4, 4] sts, K2 [2, 3, 4, 4].

Row 8: P2 [2, 3, 4, 4], *P1, yo, P2tog, P3, P2tog tbl, yo, rep from * to last 3 [3, 4, 5, 5] sts, P3 [3, 4, 5, 5].

Row 9: K3 [3, 4, 5, 5], *K1, yo, K2tog tbl, K1, K2tog, yo, K2, rep from * to last 2 [2, 3, 4, 4] sts, K2 [2, 3, 4, 4].

Row 10: P2 [2, 3, 4, 4], *P3, yo, P3tog, yo, P2, rep from * to last 3 [3, 4, 5, 5] sts, P3 [3, 4, 5, 5].

These 10 rows form patt and cont side shaping. (**Note:** When working patt, cont to work edge sts outside markers in St st and sts inside markers following the 8-st patt repeat.)

Cont in patt, shaping side seams by inc one st at each end of 9th [3rd, 3rd, 3rd, 3rd] row and every foll 12th [10th, 10th, 10th, 8th] row to 73 [91, 89, 91, 103] sts, then on every foll 10th [8th, 8th, 8th, -] row until there are 91 [93, 97, 99, -] sts, taking inc sts into St st until there are sufficient to take into patt.

Work even until sleeve measures 17 [17, 17$\frac{1}{4}$, 17$\frac{1}{4}$, 17$\frac{1}{4}$] in./43 [43, 44, 44, 44]cm, ending with RS facing for next row.

Shape top of sleeve

Keeping patt correct throughout, bind off 5 [6, 6, 7, 7] sts at beg of next 2 rows. 81 [81, 85, 85, 89] sts.

Dec one st at each end of next 5 rows, then on EOR 3 times, then on every foll 4th row until 51 [51, 55, 55, 59] sts rem.

Work 1 row, ending with RS facing for next row.

Dec one st at each end of next row and every foll alt row to 45 sts, then on foll 5 rows, ending with RS facing for next row.

Bind off rem 35 sts.

FINISHING

Block then press lightly on WS, following instructions on yarn label and avoiding ribbing.

Join shoulder seams using backstitch.

Button band

With RS facing and using size 1 (2.25mm) needles and yarn MC, pick up and knit 41 [41, 43, 43, 45] sts down left front opening edge, between neck shaping and base of front opening.

Row 1 (WS): K1, *P1, K1, rep from * to end.
Row 2: K2, *P1, K1, rep from * to last st, K1.
These 2 rows form rib.
Work 7 more rows in rib, ending with RS facing for next row.
Bind off in rib.

Buttonhole band

With RS facing and using size 1 (2.25mm) needles and yarn MC, pick up and knit 41 [41, 43, 43, 45] sts up right front opening edge, between base of front opening and neck shaping.
Work in rib as given for button band for 4 rows.
Row 5 (WS): Rib 2, *work 2tog, yo (to make a buttonhole), rib 6, rep from * 3 times more, work 2tog, yo (to make 5th buttonhole), rib to end.
Work 4 rows in rib.
Bind off in rib.

Collar

With RS facing, using size 1 (2.25mm) needles and yarn MC, and starting and ending halfway across top of bands, pick up and knit 37 [38, 38, 41, 41] sts up right side of neck, 39 [41, 41, 43, 43] sts from back, then 37 [38, 38, 41, 41] sts down left side of neck. 113 [117, 117, 125, 125] sts. Beg with row 2, work in rib as given for button band for 4 rows.
Row 5 (RS of collar, WS of body): K2, M1, rib to last 2 sts, M1, K2.
Row 6: K1, P1, rib to last 2 sts, P1, K1.

Rep last 2 rows 13 times more.
141 [145, 145, 153, 153] sts.
Work 2 more rows in patt.
Break off yarn MC and join in yarn CC.
Work 1 row in patt.
Bind off in patt.
Sew side seams. Sew sleeve seams and set in sleeves as explained on page 124.
Lay button band over buttonhole band and stitch in place at base of front opening. Sew on buttons to correspond with buttonholes.

Home Comforts

Bed Jacket • Dressing Gown

Diamond Throw • Lacy Bed Socks

Coat-Hanger Covers • Rose Button

Cushion • Buttoned Flower Bolster

Bed Jacket

If you knit nothing else in this book, you must
knit this! It is soft, luxurious, and wonderfully
cozy, whether worn as a bed jacket over a silk
nightdress or as a summery jacket. With its
copious shawl collar and wonderfully deep lace
edgings, it is straight out of the Jean Harlow era
of glamour. Make it in whichever rich shade of
Rowan's Kid Classic yarn you fancy.

BED JACKET by Jennie Atkinson

SIZES

	XS–S	M–L	
To fit bust	32–34	36–38	in.
	81–86	91–97	cm

For actual size, see diagram below.

YARN

9 [10] balls of Rowan *Kid Classic* (50g/ 1³⁄₄oz) in desired shade (Feather 828 was used here)

NEEDLES AND HOOK

Size 8 (5mm) circular knitting needle (24 in./60cm)
Pair of size 8 (5mm) knitting needles
Size F-5 (4.00mm) crochet hook

GAUGE

19 sts and 25 rows to 4 in./10cm measured over stockinette stitch using size 8 (5mm) needles.

BACK AND FRONTS

The back and fronts are worked in one piece.
Using size 8 (5mm) circular needle, cast on 25 [28] sts.

Work back and forth in rows as foll:
Row 1 (WS): K7 [8], (yo, K2tog, K7 [8]) twice.
Row 2: Cast on 4 sts, P3, (yo, P2tog, P7 [8]) twice, yo, P2tog, P6 [7]. 29 [32] sts.
Row 3: Cast on 4 sts, K2, *yo, K2tog, K7 [8], rep from * to last 4 sts, yo, K2tog, K2. 33 [36] sts.
Row 4: Cast on 5 [6] sts, P8 [9], *yo, P2tog, P7 [8], rep from * to last 3 sts, yo, P2tog, P1. 38 [42] sts.
Row 5: Cast on 5 [6] sts, K7 [8], *yo, K2tog, K7 [8], rep from * to end. 43 [48] sts.
Rep rows 2–5 seven more times, ending with RS facing for next row. 169 [188] sts.
Patt rows will now read:
Right side row: P8 [9], *yo, P2tog, P7 [8], rep from * to last 8 [9] sts, yo, P2tog, P6 [7].
Wrong side row: K7 [8], *yo, K2tog, K7 [8], rep from * to end.
Work 12 more rows in patt as set, ending with RS facing for next row.
Dec row (RS): P3, P2tog, P3 [4], *yo, P2tog, P2 [3], P2tog, P3, rep from * to

last 8 [9] sts, yo, P2tog, P2 [3], P2tog, P2. 150 [169] sts.
Next row: K6 [7], *yo, K2tog, K6 [7], rep from * to end.
Next row: P7 [8], *yo, K2tog, P6 [7], rep from * to last 7 [8] sts, yo, P2tog, P5 [6].
Work even in patt as set until jacket measures 8³⁄₄ in./22cm from cast-on edge, ending with RS facing for next row.
Divide for fronts and back
Next row (RS): Slip first 35 [39] sts onto a holder and leave for right front.
Break off yarn.
Back
With RS still facing, rejoin yarn to rem sts, work 80 [91] sts in patt, then turn and leave rem 35 [39] sts on a holder for left front.
Keeping patt correct as set throughout, work 1 row.
Underarm and sleeve shaping
Working extra sts into patt as set, cast on 2 sts at beg of next 6 rows, 2 [3] sts at beg of foll 2 rows, and 8 [9] sts at beg of foll 10 rows. 176 [199] sts.
Work even for 42 rows.
Shape upper arms and shoulders
Bind off 8 [9] sts at beg of next 18 rows.
Bind off rem 32 [37] sts.
Left front
With RS facing, rejoin yarn to 35 [39] sts on spare needle for left front.
Work 2 rows.
Shape front neck and sleeves
Next row: Cast on 2 sts, patt to last 2 sts, work 2tog.
Dec one st at neck edge on every foll 6th row 5 [3] times, then on every foll 4th row 5 [8] times *and at the same time* cast on 2 sts at beg of EOR twice and 2 [3] sts on foll alt row, then cast on 8 [9] sts at beg of EOR 5 times.
Work even until left front matches back to beg of upper arm and shoulder shaping,

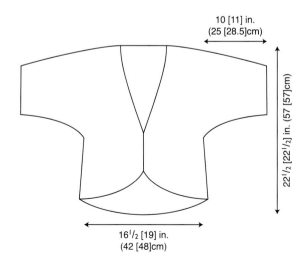

10 [11] in.
(25 [28.5]cm)

22¹⁄₂ [22¹⁄₂] in. (57 [57]cm)

16¹⁄₂ [19] in.
(42 [48]cm)

ending with RS facing for next row.
Shape upper arm and shoulder
Bind off 8 [9] sts at beg of next row and
EOR 7 times.
Work even for 1 row.
Bind off rem 8 [9] sts.
Right front
With RS facing, rejoin yarn to 35 [39] sts
on spare needle for right front.
Work 2 rows.
Shape front neck and sleeves
Next row: Work 2tog, patt to end.
Next row: Cast on 2 sts, patt to end.
Dec one st at neck edge on foll 5th row,
then on every foll 6th row 4 [2] times,
then on every foll 4th row 5 [8] times *and
at the same time* cast on 2 sts at beg of
EOR twice and 2 [3] sts on foll alt row, then
cast on 8 [9] sts at beg of EOR 5 times.
Work even until right front matches back
to beg of upper arm and shoulder
shaping, ending with *WS* row facing for
next row.
Shape upper arm and shoulder
Bind off 8 [9] sts at beg of next row and
EOR 7 times.
Work even for 1 row.
Bind off rem 8 [9] sts.

COLLAR
Collar starts at left-shoulder end.
Using size 8 (5mm) needles, cast on 5 sts.
Work 2 rows in garter st (knit every row).
Next row: Cast on 4 sts, K these 4 sts,
K to end. 9 sts.
Next row: K to end.
Rep last 2 rows 11 times, then first row
once, ending with *WS* facing for next row.
57 sts.
Next 2 rows: K25, turn, sl 1, K to end.
Next 2 rows: K45, turn, sl 1, K to end.
Next 2 rows: K25, turn, sl 1, K to end.
Next 2 rows: K to end.
Rep last 8 rows 30 [32] times more.

Next row: K to end.
Bind off 4 sts at beg of next row and
EOR 12 times.
Knit 1 row. Bind off rem 5 sts.

FINISHING
Block then press lightly on WS, following
instructions on yarn label.
Sew underarm and upper sleeve and
shoulder seams.

MAIN EDGING
Using size 8 (5mm) needles, cast on 10 sts.
Row 1: K2, (yo, K2tog) 3 times, yo, K2.
11 sts.
Row 2: K2, (yo, K1) twice, (yo, K2tog)
3 times, K1. 13 sts.
Row 3: K2, (yo, K2tog) 3 times, yo, K3, yo,
K2. 15 sts.
Row 4: K2, yo, K5, yo, K1, (yo, K2tog)
3 times, K1. 17 sts.
Row 5: K2, (yo, K2tog) 3 times, yo, skp,
K3, K2tog, yo, K2. 17 sts.
Row 6: K3, yo, skp, K1, K2tog, yo,

K2, (yo, K2tog) 3 times, K1. 17 sts.
Row 7: K2, (yo, K2tog) 3 times, K2, yo,
sl 1, K2tog, psso, yo, K4. 17 sts.
Row 8: Bind off 7 sts, K2, (yo, K2tog)
3 times, K1. 10 sts.
These 8 rows form patt and are repeated
throughout.
Cont in patt until border fits all around
outer edge of bed jacket, ending with a
row 8. Bind off.
Sew edging in place.

CUFF EDGINGS (BOTH ALIKE)
Work as given for main edging until cuff
fits around lower sleeve edging. Bind off.
Sew edgings in place.

CORD
Using size F-5 (4.00mm) crochet hook,
ch500.
Next row: 1 slip st in each ch.
Fasten off.
Thread cord through eyelets to tie under
bust.

Dressing Gown

This is the grown-up, full-size version of the Bed
Jacket on page 50 and is also knitted in the same
Kid Classic yarn. The paneled shape flares out
at the base and will make you feel like a million
dollars, keeping you warm on cold winter nights
or mornings as well.

DRESSING GOWN by Jennie Atkinson

SIZES

	XS–S	M–L	
To fit bust	32–34	36–38	in.
	81–86	91–97	cm

For actual size, see diagram opposite.

YARN

Long version
17 [19] balls of Rowan *Kid Classic*
(50g/1¾oz) in desired shade (Glacier
822 was used here)
Shorter version
16 [18] balls of Rowan *Kid Classic*
(50g/1¾oz) in desired shade

NEEDLES AND HOOK

Size 8 (5mm) circular knitting needle
(29 in./74cm)
Pair of size 8 (5mm) knitting needles
Size F-5 (4.00mm) crochet hook

GAUGE

19 sts and 25 rows to 4 in./10cm
measured over stockinette stitch using
size 8 (5mm) needles.

BACK AND FRONTS

The back and fronts are worked in one
piece.
Using size 8 (5mm) circular needle, cast
on 26 [28] sts.
Work back and forth in rows as foll:
Row 1 (WS): K12 [13], yo, K2tog, K12 [13].
Row 2: Cast on 7 sts, P6, yo, P2tog, P12
[13], yo, P2tog, P11 [12]. 33 [35] sts.
Row 3: Cast on 7 sts, K5, *yo, K2tog, K12
[13], rep from * to last 7 sts, yo, K2tog,
K5. 40 [42] sts.
Row 4: Cast on 7 [8] sts, P13 [14], *yo,
P2tog, P12 [13], rep from * to last 6 sts,
yo, P2tog, P4. 47 [50] sts.
Row 5: Cast on 7 [8] sts, K12 [13],*yo,
K2tog, K12 [13], rep from * to end. 54
[58] sts.

Rep last rows 2–5 three times, ending
with RS facing for next row.
138 [148] sts.
Working extra sts into patt as set, cast
on 2 sts at beg of next 16 [26] rows and
one st at beg of next 108 [98] rows,
ending with RS facing for next row. 278
[298] sts.
Patt rows will now read:
Right side row: P13 [14], *yo, P2tog, P12
[13], rep from * to last 13 [14] sts, yo,
P2tog, P11 [12].
Wrong side row: K12 [13], *yo, K2tog,
K12 [13], rep from * to end.
Keeping patt correct as set throughout,
work 2 rows.
Dec row 1 (RS): P6, P2tog, P5 [6], *yo,
P2tog, P5, P2tog, P5 [6], rep from * to
last 13 [14] sts, yo, P2tog, P4, P2tog,
P5 [6]. 258 [278] sts.
Next row: K11 [12], *yo, K2tog, K11
[12], rep from * to end.
Next row: P12 [13], *yo, P2tog, P11 [12],
rep from * to last 12 [13] sts, yo, P2tog,
P10 [11].
For long version only:
Work even for 21 more rows.
For short version only:
Work even for 15 more rows.
For both versions:
Dec row 2: P5, P2tog, P5 [6], *yo, P2tog,
P4 [5], P2tog, P5, rep from * to last
12 [13] sts, yo, P2tog, P4, P2tog, P4 [5].
238 [258] sts.
Next row: K10 [11], *yo, K2tog, K10
[11], rep from * to end.
Next row: P11 [12], *yo, P2tog, P10 [11],
rep from * to last 11[12] sts, yo, P2tog,
P9 [10].
For long version only:
Work even for 21 more rows.
For short version only:
Work even for 15 more rows.
For both versions:

Dec row 3: P5, P2tog, P4 [5], *yo, P2tog,
P4, P2tog, P4 [5], rep from * to last
11[12] sts, yo, P2tog, P3 [4], P2tog, P4.
218 [238] sts.
Next row: K9 [10], *yo, K2tog, K9 [10],
rep from * to end.
Next row: P10 [11], *yo, P2tog, P9 [10],
rep from * to last 10[11] sts, yo, P2tog,
P8 [9].
For long version only:
Work even for 21 more rows.
For short version only:
Work even for 15 more rows.
For both versions:
Dec row 4: P4, P2tog, P4 [5], *yo, P2tog,
P3 [4], P2tog, P4, rep from * to last
10[11] sts, yo, P2tog, P3, P2tog, P3 [4].
198 [218] sts.
Next row: K8 [9], *yo, K2tog, K8 [9], rep
from * to end.
Next row: P9 [10], *yo, P2tog, P8 [9],
rep from * to last 9 [10] sts, yo, P2tog,
P7 [8].
For long version only:
Work even for 21 more rows.
For shorter version only:
Work even for 15 more rows.
For both versions:
Dec row 5: P4, P2tog, P3 [4], *yo, P2tog,
P3 [4], P2tog, P3, rep from * to last
9 [10] sts, yo, P2tog, P2 [3], P2tog, P3.
178 [198] sts.
Next row: K7 [8], *yo, K2tog, K7 [8], rep
from * to end.
Next row: P8 [9], *yo, P2tog, P7 [8], rep
from * to last 8 [9] sts, yo, P2tog, P6 [7].
For long version only:
Work even for 21 more rows.
For short version only:
Work even for 15 more rows.
For both versions:
Dec row 6: P3 [4], P2tog, P3, *yo, P2tog,
P2 [3], P2tog, P3, rep from * to last
8 [9] sts, yo, P2tog, P2, P2tog, P2 [3].

158 [178] sts.

Next row: K6 [7], *yo, K2tog, K6 [7], rep from * to end.

Next row: P7 [8], *yo, P2tog, P6 [7], rep from * to last 7 [8] sts, yo, P2tog, P5 [6].

Cont even until long version measures 48 in./122cm (or short version measures 40 in./102cm) from cast-on edge, ending with RS facing for next row.

Divide for fronts and back

Next row (RS): Slip first 39 [44] sts onto a holder and leave for right front.

Back

With RS still facing, rejoin yarn to rem sts, work 80 [90] sts in patt, then turn and leave rem 39 [44] sts on a holder for left front.

Work 1 row.

Underarm and sleeve shaping

Working extra sts into patt, cast on 2 sts at beg of next 6 rows, 2 [3] sts at beg of foll 2 rows and 8 [9] sts at beg of foll 18 [16] rows. 240 [252] sts.

Work even for 28 [32] rows.

Shape upper arm and shoulder

Bind off 8 [9] sts at beg of next 26 [24] rows.

Bind off rem 32 [36] sts.

Left front

With right side facing, rejoin yarn to 39 [44] sts on spare needle for left front.

Work 2 rows.

Shape front neck and sleeves

Next row: Cast on 2 sts, patt to last 2 sts, work 2tog.

Dec one st at neck edge every foll 4th row 11 [10] times and then on every foll alt row 3 [6] times *and at the same time* cast on 2 sts at beg of EOR twice and 2 [3] sts at beg of next alt row, then cast on 8 [9] sts at beg of EOR 9 [8] times.

Work even until left front matches back to beg of upper arm and shoulder shaping, ending with RS facing for next row.

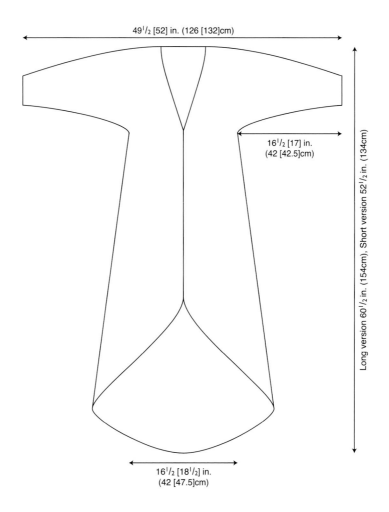

49 1/2 [52] in. (126 [132]cm)

16 1/2 [17] in. (42 [42.5]cm)

Long version 60 1/2 in. (154cm), Short version 52 1/2 in. (134cm)

16 1/2 [18 1/2] in. (42 [47.5]cm)

Shape upper arm and shoulder
Bind off 8 [9] sts at beg of next row and EOR 11 [10] times.
Work even for 1 row.
Bind off rem 8 [9] sts.

Right front
With RS facing, rejoin yarn to 39 [44] sts on spare needle for right front.
Work 2 rows.

Shape front neck and sleeves
Next row: Work 2tog, patt to end.
Next row: Cast on 2 sts, patt to end.
Dec one st at neck edge on foll 5th row, then on every foll 4th row 10 [9] times and then on every foll alt row 3 [6] times *and at the same time* cast on 2 sts at beg of EOR twice and 2 [3] sts on foll alt row, then cast on 8 [9] sts at beg of EOR 9 [8] times.
Work even until right front matches back to beg of upper arm and shoulder shaping, ending with **WS** facing for next row.

Shape upper arm and shoulder
Bind off 8 [9] sts at beg of next row and EOR 11[10] times.
Work even for 1 row.
Bind off rem 8 [9] sts.

COLLAR

Collar starts at left-shoulder end.
Using size 8 (5mm) needles, cast on 5 sts.
Work 2 rows in garter st (knit every row).
Next row: Cast on 4 sts, K these 4 sts, K to end.
Next row: K to end.
Rep last 2 rows 11 times, then first row once. 57 sts.
Next 2 rows: K25, turn, sl 1, K to end.
Next 2 rows: K45, turn, sl 1, K to end.
Next 2 rows: K25, turn, sl 1, K to end.
Next 2 rows: K to end.
Rep last 8 rows 30 [32] times.

Next row: K to end.
Bind off 4 sts at beg of next row and EOR 12 times.
Knit 1 row.
Bind off rem 5 sts.

FINISHING

Block then press lightly on WS, following instructions on yarn label.
Join underarm and upper sleeve and shoulder seams.

MAIN EDGING

Using size 8 (5mm) needles, cast on 10 sts.
Row 1: K2, (yo, K2tog) 3 times, yo, K2. 11 sts.
Row 2: K2, (yo, K1) twice, (yo, K2tog) 3 times, K1. 13 sts.
Row 3: K2, (yo, K2tog) 3 times, yo, K3, yo, K2. 15 sts.
Row 4: K2, yo, K5, yo, K1, (yo, K2tog) 3 times, K1. 17 sts.
Row 5: K2, (yo, K2tog) 3 times, yo, skp, K3, K2tog, yo, K2. 17 sts.
Row 6: K3, yo, skp, K1, K2tog, yo, K2, (yo, K2tog) 3 times, K1. 17 sts.
Row 7: K2, (yo, K2tog) 3 times, K2, yo, sl 1, K2tog, psso, yo, K4. 17 sts.
Row 8: Bind off 7 sts, K2, (yo, K2tog) 3 times, K1. 10 sts.
These 8 rows form patt and are repeated throughout.
Cont in patt until border fits all around outer edge of dressing gown, ending with a row 8.
Bind off.
Sew edging in place.

CUFF EDGINGS (BOTH ALIKE)

Work as given for main edging until cuff fits around lower sleeve edging.
Bind off.
Sew edgings in place.

CORD

Using size F-5 (4.00mm) crochet hook, ch500.
Next row: 1 slip st in each ch.
Fasten off.
Thread cord through eyelets to tie under bust.

Diamond Throw

Knitted in Rowan's cashmere-mix yarn, this pastel throw is the ultimate comfort item. Wrap it around when you lie on the sofa, or have it on the end of your bed for extra warmth at night. The diamond eyelet pattern gives it a great all-over texture, and the simple crochet-loop edging and fringing add a touch of luxury.

DIAMOND THROW by Jennie Atkinson

FINISHED SIZE

Finished throw measures 42½ in./108cm wide by 55 in./140cm long, excluding edging.

YARN

20 balls of Rowan *RYC Baby Cashsoft DK* (50g/1¾oz) in desired shade (Chicory 804 was used here)

NEEDLES AND HOOK

Pair of size 6 (4mm) knitting needles
Size F-5 (4.00mm) crochet hook

GAUGE

22 sts and 30 rows to 4 in./10cm measured over stockinette stitch using size 6 (4mm) needles.

CENTER PANEL

Using size 6 (4mm) needles, cast on 35 sts.
Row 1 and every odd-numbered row (WS): K to end.
Row 2: K2, (yo, K2tog) twice, K4, (K2tog, yo) twice, K1, yo, skp, K1, K2tog, yo, K1, (yo, skp) twice, K4, (yo, K2tog) twice, K2.
Row 4: K2, (yo, K2tog) twice, K3, (K2tog, yo) twice, K1, yo, skp, yo, sl 1, K2tog, psso, yo, K2tog, yo, K1, (yo, skp) twice, K3, (yo, K2tog) twice, K2.
Row 6: K2, (yo, K2tog) twice, K2, *(K2tog, yo) twice, K1, (yo, skp) twice, K1, rep from * once, K1, (yo, K2tog) twice, K2.
Row 8: K2, (yo, K2tog) twice, K1, (K2tog, yo) twice, K3, yo, skp, yo, sl 1, K2tog, psso, yo, K2tog, yo, K3, (yo, skp) twice, K1, (yo, K2tog) twice, K2.
Row 10: K2, (yo, K2tog) twice, *K1, (yo, skp) twice, K2, (K2tog, yo) twice, rep from * once, K1, (yo, K2tog) twice, K2.

Row 12: K2, (yo, K2tog) twice, K2, (yo, skp) twice, (K2tog, yo) twice, K3, (yo, skp) twice, (K2tog, yo) twice, K2, (yo, K2tog) twice, K2.
Row 14: K2, (yo, K2tog) twice, K3, yo, skp, (K2tog, yo) twice, K1, yo, sl 1, K2tog, psso, yo, K1, (yo, skp) twice, K2tog, yo, K3, (yo, K2tog) twice, K2.
These 14 rows form patt and are repeated throughout.
Cont in patt until panel measures 55 in./140cm from cast-on edge, ending with a row 14.
Bind off.

SIDE PANELS (MAKE 2)

Using size 6 (4mm) needles, cast on 98 sts.
Row 1 and every odd-numbered row (WS): K to end.
Row 2: K7, *K2tog, yo, K1, yo, K2tog, K11, rep from * ending last rep K6.
Row 4: K6, *K2tog, yo, K3, yo, K2tog, K9, rep from * ending last rep K5.
Row 6: K5, *K2tog, yo, K5, yo, K2tog, K7, rep from * ending last rep K4.
Row 8: K4, *K2tog, yo, K7, yo, K2tog, K5, rep from * ending last rep K3.
Row 10: K3, *K2tog, yo, K9, yo, K2tog, K3, rep from * ending last rep K2.
Row 12: K1, *K1, K2tog, yo, K11, yo, K2tog, rep from * to last st, K1.
Row 14: K1, *K1, yo, K2tog, K11, K2tog, yo, rep from * to last st, K1.
Row 16: Rep row 12.
Row 18: Rep row 10.
Row 20: Rep row 8.
Row 22: Rep row 6.
Row 24: Rep row 4.
These 24 rows form patt and are repeated throughout.
Cont in patt until panel measures 55 in./140cm from cast-on edge.
Bind off.

FINISHING

Block then press lightly on WS, following instructions on yarn label.
Sew panels together.

CROCHET BORDER

With RS facing and using size F-5 (4.00mm) crochet hook, attach yarn to any corner.
Round 1 (RS): Work 1sc in corner, *ch8, work 1sc in edge of blanket 1½ in./4cm from previous sc, rep from * all around blanket, working 1sc in each corner, join with a slip st in first sc. Do not turn at end of rounds, but work with RS always facing.
Round 2: 1 slip st in each of first 4ch, 1sc in first 8ch sp, *ch8, 1sc in next ch sp, rep from *, ending with ch8, join with a slip st in first sc.
Mark each corner 8ch sp and cont as foll:
Round 3: 1 slip st in each of first 4ch, 1sc in first 8ch sp, *ch8, 1sc in next ch sp, rep from * to first corner ch sp, (ch8, 1sc in corner ch sp) twice, rep from * 3 times more, ch8, join with a slip st in first sc.
Fasten off.

FRINGE

Cut remaining yarn into 8 in./20cm lengths. Knot six lengths into each 8ch sp around outside edge to form fringe.

Lacy Bed Socks

Soft and lacy, these long-length bed socks offer just the right amount of warmth and comfort, and are pretty enough to wear out, too. Knitted in the round on four double-pointed needles in Rowan's cashmere-mix yarn, they're just the thing to accompany the knitted Dressing Gown on page 55 on cold nights.

LACY BED SOCKS by Jennie Atkinson

SIZE
One size to fit woman's shoe sizes 5–8.

YARN
3 balls of Rowan *RYC Cashsoft 4-Ply* (50g/1³/₄oz) in desired shade (Rose Lake 421 was used here)

NEEDLES
Set of four size 3 (3.25mm) double-pointed knitting needles

EXTRAS
44 in./112cm of narrow satin ribbon

GAUGE
28 sts and 36 rows to 4 in./10cm measured over stockinette stitch using size 3 (3.25mm) needles.

TO MAKE SOCKS
Using set of four size 3 (3.25mm) double-pointed needles, cast on 60 sts onto one needle. Then distribute sts evenly on 3 needles (20 sts on each needle).
Round 1 (RS): K to end.
Rep last round 3 times.
Next round (picot round): *K2tog, yo, rep from * to end of round.
Knit 6 rounds.
Purl 1 round.
Next round (eyelet round): *K3, yo, K2tog, rep from * to end of round.
Purl 1 round, decreasing 4 sts evenly. 56 sts.
Work in patt as foll:
Patt round 1: *K2, yo, skp, yo, sl 1, K2tog, psso, yo, rep from * to end of round.
Patt round 2: *P2tog, yo, P2, K3, rep from * to end.
Patt round 3: *K2, yo, skp, K3, rep from * to end.
Patt round 4: Rep round 2.

These 4 rounds form patt.
Cont in patt until sock measures 12 in./30cm from picot round, ending with a patt round 2 or patt round 4. Break off yarn.
Shape heel
Slip next 14 sts onto first needle, next 14 sts onto second needle, next 14 sts onto third needle, and last 14 sts onto end of first needle.
Rejoin yarn to beg of first needle and work in rows as foll:
Next row (RS): K27, turn.
Next row: Sl 1 purlwise, P25, turn.
Next row: Sl 1 purlwise, K24, turn.
Next row: Sl 1 purlwise, P23, turn.
Cont in this way, working one st less on every row until foll rows have been worked:
Next row: Sl 1 purlwise, K14, turn.
Next row: Sl 1 purlwise, P13, turn.
Next row: Sl 1 purlwise, K14, turn.
Cont in this way, working one st more on every row until foll row has been worked:
Next row: Sl 1 purlwise, P27, turn.
Break off yarn.
Arrange sts so that first 17 sts are on first needle, "center" 21 sts are on second needle, and last 18 sts on third needle.
Cont to work center 21 sts in patt and rem sts in St st, work in rounds until sock measures 7¹/₂ in./19cm from back of heel. Break off yarn.
Slip next 14 sts onto first needle, next 14 sts onto second needle, next 14 sts onto third needle, and last 14 sts onto end of first needle.
Shape toe
Rejoin yarn to beg of first needle and shape toe as foll:
Next round: (K2, skp, K20, K2tog, K2) twice.

Next round: K to end.
Next round: (K2, skp, K18, K2tog, K2) twice.
Next round: K to end.
Next round: (K2, skp, K16, K2tog, K2) twice.
Next round: K to end.
Cont in rounds decreasing on every alt round as set until foll round has been worked.
Next round: (K2, skp, K6, K2tog, K2) twice.
Slip first 12 sts onto one needle and rem 12 sts onto a second needle, then fold sock inside out and bind off both layers together by inserting needle through one st on each needle while binding off.
Cut ribbon in half and thread one piece through eyelets at top of each sock.
Then tie in a bow as in photograph.

Hanger Covers

If you have some nice silk dresses or tops, it
makes sense to treat them with respect and hang
them on decorated padded hangers. These are so
pretty they deserve to be on show outside the
closet. Knit them with or without a pretty lace
edging, in a variety of ice cream colors. Go on,
spoil yourself—or a friend. Make a white one as a
wedding gift for the bride's dress. For alternatives
to the knitted edging, try the simple crochet
ones on pages 120 and 121.

HANGER COVERS by Jennie Atkinson

FINISHED SIZE
Finished hanger covers will fit any length hanger with padded arms approximately 4½ in./11.5cm in diameter.

YARN
1 ball of Jaeger *Siena* (50g/1¾ oz) for each cover in desired shade (Blush 417 was used here for Lace Cover with Edging and Phlox 422 for Plain Lace Cover)

NEEDLES
Pair each of size 2 (2.75mm) and size 3 (3mm) knitting needles

EXTRAS
Hanger, with white padded arms about 4½ in./11.5cm in diameter
12 in./30cm of ⅜ in./7mm wide satin ribbon in desired shade

GAUGE
Approximately 29 sts to 4½ in./11.5cm measured over lace pattern using size 2 (2.75mm) needles.

LACE COVER WITH EDGING

TO MAKE COVER
Using size 2 (2.75mm) needles, cast on 29 sts.
Row 1: P to end.
Row 2: (K1, P1, K1) all into first st, *sl 1, P2tog, psso, (K1, P1, K1) all into next st, rep from * to end. 31 sts.
Row 3: P to end.
Row 4: *Sl 1, P2tog, psso, (K1, P1, K1) all into next st, rep from * to last 3 sts, sl 1, P2tog, psso. (29 sts)
These 4 rows form patt and are repeated throughout.
Work in patt until required length for hanger (cover shown fits a 17 in./43cm hanger), ending with a row 2 or 4.
(**Note:** The lace fabric is stretchy, so test around hanger before binding off.)
Bind off purlwise.

EDGING
Using size 3 (3mm) needles, cast on 6 sts.
Row 1: K2, yo, K2tog, yo, K2. 7 sts.
Row 2: K2, (yo, K1) twice, yo, K2tog, K1. 9 sts.
Row 3: K2, yo, K2tog, yo, K3, yo, K2. 11 sts.
Row 4: K2, yo, K5, yo, K1, yo, K2tog, K1. 13 sts.
Row 5: K2, yo, K2tog, yo, skp, K3, K2tog, yo, K2.
Row 6: K3, yo, skp, K1, K2tog, yo, K2, yo, K2tog, K1.
Row 7: K2, yo, K2tog, K2, yo, sl 1, K2tog, psso, yo, K4.
Row 8: Bind off 7 sts, K2, yo, K2tog, K1. 6 sts.
These 8 rows form patt and are repeated throughout.
Work in patt until edging fits length of cover, ending with a row 8.
Bind off.

FINISHING
Do NOT press.
Place cover over hanger, slipping hook through center. Sew row-end edges together, then pinch ends together so that seam just worked is in center and sew end seams. Sew edging in place along bottom seam. Tie ribbon around hook.

PLAIN LACE COVER

TO MAKE COVER
Make exactly as for Lace Cover with Edging, but omit edging.

Rose Button Cushion

Here's a chance to practice your colorwork
knitting. This eye-catching, softly colored rose-
motif cushion is the ultimate boudoir accessory.
Knitted in Rowan's merino wool yarn, it is lavishly
decorated with buttons and beads on both the
front and the back. If you need them, there are
useful tips for color knitting and following a chart
on pages 122 and 124.

ROSE BUTTON CUSHION by Lois Daykin

FINISHED SIZE
Finished cushion measures 17½ in./
45cm square.

YARN
Rowan *4-Ply Soft* (50g/1¾oz) in 2 desired
shades, or shades used here as foll:

A Whisper 370   6 balls
B Day Dream 378   1 ball

Rowan *Kidsilk Haze* (25g/1oz) in 4 desired
shades, or shades used here as foll:

C Dewberry 600   1 ball
D Drab 588   1 ball
E Majestic 589   1 ball
F Pearl 590   1 ball

Note: Use *Kidsilk Haze* DOUBLE
throughout.

NEEDLES
Pair of size 3 (3.25mm) knitting needles

EXTRAS
Pillow form 18 in./45cm square
9mm mother-of-pearl buttons, 60
(Rowan no. 00333)
3mm round glass beads, 580, in gold
(Rowan no. 01005)
3mm round glass beads, 500, in silver
(Rowan no. 01008)
Matching sewing thread for sewing on
buttons and beads

GAUGE
28 sts and 36 rows to 4 in./10cm
measured over stockinette stitch using
size 3 (3.25mm) needles.

FRONT
Using size 3 (3.25mm) needles and yarn
A, cast on 146 sts.
Row 1 (RS): *K1, P1, rep from * to end.
Row 2: *P1, K1, rep from * to end.
These 2 rows form seed st.
Work 15 more rows in seed st, ending

with **WS** facing for next row.
Row 18 (WS): Seed st 11 sts, P to last
11 sts, seed st 11 sts.
Row 19: Seed st 11 sts, K to last 11 sts,
seed st 11 sts.
Rows 20 to 27: Rep rows 18 and 19 four
times.
Row 28: Rep row 18.
Place chart
Joining in and breaking off colors as
required and using the intarsia technique
as explained on pages 122 and 124,
place chart as foll:
Row 29 (RS): Seed st 11 sts, work next
124 sts as row 1 of chart, seed st 11 sts.
Row 30: Seed st 11 sts, work next 124
sts as row 2 of chart, seed st 11 sts.
These 2 rows set position of chart.
Cont as set until all 155 rows of chart
have been completed, ending with **WS**
facing for next row.
Rows 184 to 193: Rep rows 18 and 19
five times.
Row 194: Rep row 18.
Rows 195 to 210: Rep rows 1 and 2
eight times.
Row 211: Rep row 1.
Bind off in seed st.

BACK
Using size 3 (3.25mm) needles and yarn
A, cast on 124 sts.
Beg with a P row, work in St st for 11
rows, ending with RS facing for next row.
Place chart
Joining in and breaking off colors as
required and using the intarsia technique
as explained on pages 122 and 124, cont
in patt foll chart until all 155 rows of
chart have been completed, ending with
WS facing for next row.
Beg with a P row, work in St st for 11
rows, ending with RS facing for next row.
Bind off.

FINISHING
Block then press lightly on WS, following
instructions on yarn label.
Using photograph as a guide and
matching thread, sew a line of buttons
to St st band around each smaller motif,
attaching each button with two gold
beads. Sew a line of gold beads around
both sides of the seed st band inside this
St st band, then a line of silver beads
around outer edge of seed st band
outside band with buttons. Sew a line of
gold beads around inner edge of seed st
band around larger motif, and a line of
silver beads around outer edge of this
seed st band.
Lay back on top of front with wrong
sides together, positioning so that outer
edge of back matches inner edge of seed
st border of front. Sew pieces together
along three sides. Insert pillow form and
sew fourth side closed.

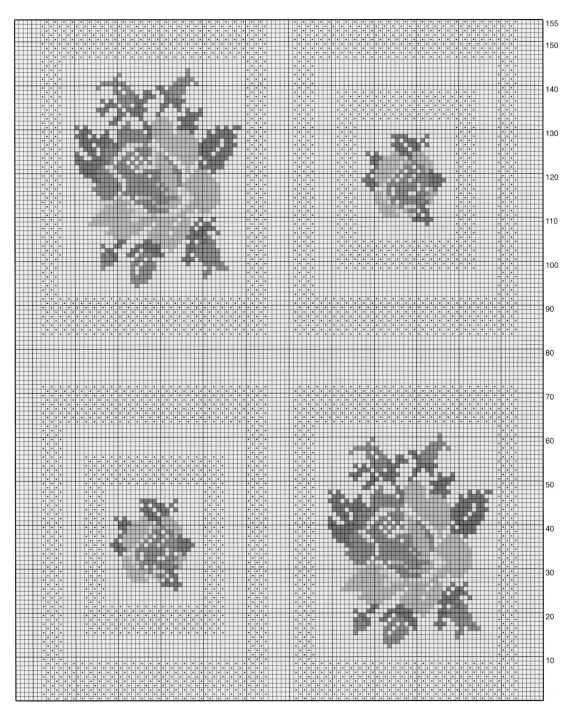

155
150
140
130
120
110
100
90
80
70
60
50
40
30
20
10

Key

☐ A   ▨ B   ▪ C   ▨ D   ▨ E   ☐ F   ☐ A - P on RS,
                                                    K on WS
    └─────────────────────────────┘
         K on RS, P on WS

Buttoned Flower Bolster

This is a girlie dream come true. The combination of soft colors, lace, buttons, and beads would give any bedroom a feminine touch, and just a hint of Victoriana. Match it with the Rose Button Cushion on page 73 for the full effect. To put your personal stamp on these confections, take your time picking out some unique buttons and beads.

BUTTONED FLOWER BOLSTER by Lois Daykin

FINISHED SIZE
Finished bolster measures approximately
8 in./20cm in diameter by 19½ in./50cm
long.

YARN
Rowan *4-Ply Cotton* (50g/1¾oz) in 4
desired shades, or shades used here as foll:

A	Opaque 112	2 balls
B	Bleached 113	1 ball
C	Fresh 131	2 balls
D	Ripple 121	2 balls

NEEDLES
Pair of size 2 (3mm) knitting needles

EXTRAS
¾ yd/70cm of 44 in./112cm wide fabric
and matching sewing thread for making
bolster cushion
Polyfil for filling cushion
5½ yd/5m of narrow satin ribbon
Selection of beads and mother-of-pearl
buttons for decoration and matching
sewing thread

GAUGE
28 sts and 38 rows to 4 in./10cm
measured over stockinette stitch using
size 2 (3mm) needles.

MAIN SECTION
Using size 2 (3mm) needles, cast on as foll:
6 sts using yarn B, 23 sts using yarn C,
5 sts using yarn B, 44 sts using yarn D,
5 sts using yarn B, 23 sts using yarn C,
and 6 sts using yarn B. 112 sts.
Using intarsia technique as explained on
pages 122 and 124, cont in patt as foll:
Row 1 (RS): Using yarn B, K1, *using
yarn B K2tog, yo, K1, yo, skp, using yarn
C K3, K2tog, yo, K1, yo, skp, K3, yo, skp,
K2, K2tog, yo, K1, yo, skp, K3, using yarn
B K2tog, yo, K1, yo, skp,* using yarn D

K44, rep from * to * once more, using
yarn B K1.
Row 2 and every even-numbered row:
Using yarn B P6, using yarn C P23, using
yarn B P5, using yarn D P44, using yarn B
P5, using yarn C P23, using yarn B P6.
Row 3: Using yarn B, K1, *using yarn B
K2tog, yo, K1, yo, skp, using yarn C K3,
(K2tog, yo, K1, yo, skp, K1) 3 times, K2,
using yarn B K2tog, yo, K1, yo, skp,*
using yarn D K44, rep from * to * once
more, using yarn B K1.
Row 5: Using yarn B, K1, *using yarn B
K2tog, yo, K1, yo, skp, using yarn C K3,
K2tog, yo, K1, yo, skp, K2tog, yo, K3, yo,
skp, K2tog, yo, K1, yo, skp, K3, using yarn
B K2tog, yo, K1, yo, skp,* using yarn D
K44, rep from * to * once more, using
yarn B K1.
Row 6: Rep row 2.
These 6 rows form patt.
Cont in patt until main section measures
24¾ in./63cm, ending after patt row 6
and with RS facing for next row.
Bind off.

ENDS (MAKE 2)
Using size 2 (3mm) needles and yarn A,
cast on 25 sts.
Row 1 (RS): sl 1, K19, yo, P2tog, K1, yo,
K2. 26 sts.
Row 2: K4, yo, P2tog, K18, turn.
Row 3: sl 1, K17, yo, P2tog, K2, yo, K2.
Row 4: K5, yo, P2tog, K16, turn.
Row 5: Sl 1, K15, yo, P2tog, K3, yo, K2.
Row 6: K6, yo, P2tog, K14, turn.
Row 7: Sl 1, K13, yo, P2tog, K2tog, (yo)
twice, K2, yo, K2.
Row 8: K5, (K1, P1) into double yo of
previous row, K1, yo, P2tog, K12, turn.
Row 9: Sl 1, K11, yo, P2tog, K8.
Row 10: Bind off 5 sts, K until there are
3 sts on right needle, yo, P2tog, K10, turn.
Row 11: Sl 1, K9, yo, P2tog, K1, yo, K2.

Row 12: K4, yo, P2tog, K8, turn.
Row 13: Sl 1, K7, yo, P2tog, K2, yo, K2.
Row 14: K5, yo, P2tog, K6, turn.
Row 15: Sl 1, K5, yo, P2tog, K3, yo, K2.
Row 16: K6, yo, P2tog, K4, turn.
Row 17: Sl 1, K3, yo, P2tog, K2tog, (yo)
twice, K2, yo, K2.
Row 18: K5, (K1, P1) into double yo of
previous row, K1, yo, P2tog, K2, turn.
Row 19: Sl 1, K1, yo, P2tog, K8.
Row 20: Bind off 5 sts, K until there are
3 sts on right needle, yo, P2tog, K2, (yo,
K2tog) 8 times, K2.
Rep last 20 rows 15 times.
Bind off.

LARGE PETALS (MAKE 5)
Using size 2 (3mm) needles and yarn D,
cast on 3 sts.
Row 1 (RS): K1, (yo, K1) twice. 5 sts.
Row 2 and every even-numbered row:
P to end.
Row 3: K2, yo, K1, yo, K2. 7 sts.
Row 5: K3, yo, K1, yo, K3. 9 sts.
Row 7: K4, yo, K1, yo, K4. 11 sts.
Row 9: Skp, K3, yo, K1, yo, K3, K2tog.
Row 11: Rep row 9.
Row 13: Skp, K2, sl 1, K2tog, psso, K2,
K2tog. 7 sts.
Row 15: Skp, sl 1, K2tog, psso, K2tog.
3 sts.
Row 17: Sl 1, K2tog, psso and fasten off.

SMALL PETALS (MAKE 5)
Using size 2 (3mm) needles and yarn A,
cast on 3 sts.
Row 1 (RS): K1, (yo, K1) twice. 5 sts.
Row 2 and every even-numbered row:
Purl.
Row 3: K2, yo, K1, yo, K2. 7 sts.
Row 5: K3, yo, K1, yo, K3. 9 sts.
Row 7: K3, sl 1, K2tog, psso, K3. 7 sts.
Row 9: Skp, sl 1, K2tog, psso, K2tog. 3 sts.
Row 11: Sl 1, K2tog, psso and fasten off.

FINISHING

Block then press lightly on WS, following instructions on yarn label.

Bolster cushion

To make bolster cushion, cut two circles of fabric 9 in./23cm in diameter, and a rectangle of fabric 20½ in./53cm wide by 26 in./66cm long. (Seam allowances of ½ in./1.5cm are included in these dimensions.) Sew together two shorter edges of rectangle to form a tube, leaving an opening. Then sew two circles of fabric to ends of this tube, and turn cover right side out. Insert filling so that cushion is firmly filled and sew opening closed.

Knitted cover

Sew together cast-on and bound-off ends of knitted main section and end pieces. Sew one end piece to row-end edge of main section along "bar" inside the two concentric rings of eyelet holes just inside chevron edging. Sew other end piece to other end of main section in same way, inserting cushion before sewing seam closed.

Using photograph as a guide, sew large and small petals to main section to form a flower shape. Thread ribbon through eyelet holes of stripes in yarn C as in photograph, crossing ribbon every 14 rows. Sew buttons and beads to center of stripes in yarn B, and to petals and to center of flower shape to form flower center.

Little Extras

Crochet Necklace • Crochet Choker

Crochet Belt • Crochet Shawl

Crochet Motif Bag • Lace Shawl

Button Crochet Belt • Crochet Cap

Buttoned Bag

Crochet Necklace, Choker, and Belt

If you want to try out crochet, then here is your chance to get going. Make any one of these great quick-and-easy crochet accessories for yourself. Worked in Rowan's slinky Lurex Shimmer metallic yarn, with the addition of sparkly glass beads, they will add a touch of instant glamour to any outfit, and some originality, too.

CROCHET NECKLACE by Jennie Atkinson

FINISHED SIZE
Finished necklace measures 14½ in./
37cm long and 1½ in./4cm wide across
beaded loop section.

YARN
1 ball of Rowan *Lurex Shimmer* (25g/1oz)
in desired shade (Copper 330 was used
here)

HOOK
Size D-3 (3.00mm) crochet hook

EXTRAS
11 small beads: 6mm transparent
faceted glass beads in pale copper (6)
and 6mm transparent faceted glass
beads in pale green (5)
8 large beads: 8mm transparent faceted
glass beads in pale copper

GAUGE
Working to an exact gauge is not
essential for this necklace.

TO MAKE NECKLACE
Thread 11 small beads onto yarn,
starting with a pale copper bead and
alternating the colors.
Using size D-3 (3.00mm) hook, ch122.
Necklace row 1 (RS): Work 1 slip st in
10th ch from hook, 1 slip st in each of
next 24ch, ch3, slide bead up to hook,
ch3, skip next 2ch, 1 slip st in next ch,
*ch6, skip next 2ch, 1 slip st in next ch,
ch3, slide bead up to hook, ch3, skip next
2ch, 1 slip st in next ch, rep from * 9
times more (21 6ch loops made), 1 slip
st in each of rem 24ch. Do not turn and
do not break off yarn.
Make bobble button at end of last row
as foll:
Ch4 and join with a slip st in first ch to
form a ring.

Bobble round 1 (RS): Ch1, 8sc in ring.
Do not turn at end of rounds, but work
with RS always facing.
Bobble round 2: 1sc in each of 8sc of
previous round.
Bobble round 3: (Skip 1sc, 1sc in next
sc) 4 times.
Fasten off.
Thread 5 large beads onto yarn, return to
loops on necklace and cont as foll:
Necklace row 2: With RS facing, rejoin
yarn with a slip st in 2nd 6ch loop of
previous necklace row, ch5, slide bead up
to hook, ch5, skip next 6ch loop, 1 slip st
in next loop, *ch10, skip next loop, 1 slip
st in next loop, ch5, slide bead up to

hook, ch5, skip next loop, 1 slip st in next
loop, rep from * to last loop. Do not
turn. 9 10ch loops.
Fasten off.
Thread 3 large beads onto yarn.
Necklace row 3: With RS facing, rejoin
yarn with a slip st in 2nd 10ch loop of
previous row, ch10, slide bead up to
hook, ch10, skip next 10ch loop, 1 slip st
in next loop, ch14, slide bead up to hook,
ch14, skip next 10ch loop, 1 slip st in
next loop, ch10, slide bead up to hook,
ch10, skip next 10ch loop, 1 slip st in
next loop.
Fasten off.
Weave in loose ends.

CROCHET CHOKER by Jennie Atkinson

FINISHED SIZE

Finished choker measures approximately 9¼ in./23.5cm long (excluding ties at each end) by 2¼ in./5.5cm wide.

YARN

1 ball of Rowan *Lurex Shimmer* (25g/1oz) in desired shade (Copper 330 was used here)

HOOK

Size D-3 (3.00mm) crochet hook

EXTRAS

116 assorted 3–4mm glass beads (mostly transparent beads with metallic cores and some black)

GAUGE

Working to an exact gauge is not essential for this choker.

TO MAKE CHOKER

Thread 59 beads onto yarn.

Using size D-3 (3.00mm) hook, ch61.

Row 1 (RS) 1sc in 2nd ch from hook, 1sc in each of rem 59ch. Turn. 60sc.

Row 2 Ch2 (to count as first hdc), skip first sc, *1hdc in next sc, rep from * to end. Turn. 60 sts.

Row 3 Ch3 (to count as first dc), skip first hdc, *1dc in next hdc, rep from * to end, 1dc in 2nd of 2ch at end of row. Turn.

Row 4 Ch4 (to count as first tr), slide bead up to hook, skip first dc, 1tr in next dc, *slide bead up to hook, 1tr in next dc, rep from * to end, slide bead up to hook, 1tr in 3rd of 3ch at end of row.

(**Note:** Beads worked in way described on this WS row will sit on RS of choker.)

Row 5 Ch3 (to count as first dc), skip first tr, *1dc in next tr, rep from * to end, 1dc in 4th of 4ch at end of row. Turn.

Row 6 Ch1, 1sc in first dc, *1sc in next dc, rep from * to end, 1sc in 3rd of 3ch. Turn.

CROCHET BELT by Jennie Atkinson

Row 7 *Ch5, skip 2sc, 1sc in next sc, rep from * to end. Turn. 20 5ch loops.
Fasten off.
Thread 57 beads onto yarn.
Row 8 With WS facing, rejoin yarn with a slip st in first 5ch loop of previous row, *ch4, slide 3 beads up to hook, ch4, 1sc in next loop, rep from * to end.
Fasten off.

FINISHING
Weave in loose ends.
Ties
Using size D-3 (3.00mm) hook, join yarn with a slip st in one corner of one end of choker and work chain sts until tie is approximately 8³/₄ in./22cm long.
Fasten off.
Work a tie in same way at other corner at same end of choker, then a third tie equally spaced between first two.
Knot each of three ties at end.
Work three ties at other end of choker in same way.
Weave in any rem loose ends.

FINISHED SIZE
Finished belt measures approximately 43 in./109cm long and 2 in./5cm wide across widest part of beaded loop section.

YARN
1 ball of Rowan *Lurex Shimmer* (25g/1oz) in desired shade (Copper 330 was used here)

HOOK
Size D-3 (3.00mm) crochet hook

EXTRAS
6mm transparent faceted glass beads, 93, in brown (to match metallic yarn)

GAUGE
Working to an exact gauge is not essential for this belt.

TO MAKE BELT
Thread 35 beads onto yarn.
Using size D-3 (3.00mm) hook, ch361.
Row 1 (RS): Slide bead up to hook, 1 slip st in 2nd ch from hook, 1 slip st in each of next 82ch, ch3, slide bead up to hook, ch3, skip next 2ch, 1 slip st in next ch, *ch6, skip next 2ch, 1 slip st in next ch, ch3, slide bead up to hook, ch3, skip next 2ch, 1 slip st in next ch, rep from * 31 times more, 1 slip st in each of rem 82ch, slide last bead up to hook, 1 slip st in same ch as last slip st. Do not turn. 65 6ch loops.
Fasten off.
Thread 16 beads onto yarn.
Row 2: With RS facing, rejoin yarn with a slip st in 2nd 6ch loop of previous row, ch6, slide bead up to hook, ch6, skip next 6ch loop, 1 slip st in next loop, *ch12, skip next loop, 1 slip st in next loop, ch6, slide bead up to hook, ch6, skip next loop, 1 slip st in next loop, rep from * to last loop. Do not turn. 31 12ch loops.
Fasten off.
Thread 42 beads onto yarn.
Row 3: With RS facing, rejoin yarn with a slip st in 2nd 12ch loop of previous row, *ch12, slide 3 beads up to hook, ch12, skip next 12ch loop, 1 slip st in next loop, rep from * to last loop.
Fasten off.
Weave in loose ends.

Crochet Shawl

If you have been accustomed to seeing afghans
in lumpy yarns and contrasting colors, this
exquisitely soft shawl in muted hues is an eye
opener. It looks and feels exquisite, and is
both light and warm to the touch. The simple
multicolored, silk-and-mohair motifs are made
separately then crocheted together and edged
with fringe. The instructions on page 114 explain
how to start each crochet square.

CROCHET SHAWL by Kim Hargreaves

FINISHED SIZE

Finished shawl measures 17 in./43cm wide by 67 in./170cm long, excluding fringe.

YARN

Rowan *Kidsilk Haze* (25g/1oz) in 6 desired shades, or shades used here as foll:

A	Pearl 590	1 ball
B	Majestic 589	2 balls
C	Grace 580	1 ball
D	Meadow 581	1 ball
E	Drab 588	1 ball
F	Dewberry 600	1 ball

CROCHET HOOK

Size D-3 (3.00mm) crochet hook

GAUGE

One motif measures 3¼ in./8.5cm square using size D-3 (3.00mm) hook.

SPECIAL ABBREVIATION

dc2tog worked over 4 sts = *yo, insert hook in next dc, yo and draw loop through, yo and draw through 2 loops*, skip 2dc, rep from * to * once more, yo and draw through all 3 loops on hook.

BASIC MOTIF

Using size D-3 (3.00mm) hook and first color, ch10 and join with a slip st in first ch to form a ring.
Round 1 (RS): Ch3 (to count as first dc), 31dc in ring, join with a slip st in 3rd of 3ch at beg of round. Do not turn at end of rounds, but work with RS always facing.
Round 2: (Ch7, skip 3dc, 1 slip st in next dc) 7 times, ch3, skip 3dc, 1tr in next dc. Break off first color and join in 2nd color.
Round 3: Ch3 (to count as 1dc), 6dc in top of tr at end of previous round, skip 3ch, *7dc in next ch, skip (3ch, 1 slip st and 3ch), rep from * to end, join with a slip st in 3rd of 3ch at beg of round.
Round 4: 1 slip st in next dc, ch6 (to count as 1dc and 3ch), *skip 1dc, (1tr, ch5, 1tr) all in next dc, ch3, skip 1dc, dc2tog over next 4dc, ch3, skip 1dc, 1sc in next dc, ch3, skip 1dc**, dc2tog over next 4dc, ch3, rep from * to end, ending last rep at **, 1dc in next dc, join with a slip st in 3rd of 6ch at beg of round. Break off 2nd color and join in 3rd color.
Round 5: Ch1 (does NOT count as st), 1sc in same place slip st was worked at end of previous round, *3sc in next ch sp, 1sc in next tr, 6sc in next ch sp, 1sc in next tr, 3sc in next ch sp, 1sc in next dc2tog, 3sc in next ch sp, 1sc in next sc, 3sc in next ch sp**, 1sc in next dc2tog, rep from * to end, ending last rep at **, join with a slip st in first sc.
Fasten off.
Finished basic motif is a square, with 23sc along each side.

TO MAKE SHAWL

Using colors of yarn at random, make 100 basic motifs.
Join motifs to form a rectangle five motifs wide and 20 motifs long as foll:
Holding motifs WS together and using yarn B, work a row of sc along edge of motifs, inserting hook through corresponding sc of both edges.
When all motifs are joined, using yarn B work one round of sc all around entire outer edge, ending with a slip st in first sc.
Fasten off.

FINISHING

Do NOT press.
Cut 13¾ in./35cm lengths of yarn B and knot groups of five of these lengths through each ch sp along ends of shawl to form fringe.

Crochet Motif Bag

This is a great project for novice crocheters. The bag base is knitted in quick and easy stockinette stitch, and you add the crochet motifs afterward. A pretty matching satin ribbon right around the bag and tied in a bow adds a feminine detail. For more choice of motifs, turn to the showstopping ones on pages 116–119.

CROCHET MOTIF BAG by Martin Storey

FINISHED SIZE

Finished bag measures 11½ in./29cm wide by 8½ in./22cm deep.

YARN

Rowan *4-Ply Cotton* (50g/1¾oz) in 3 desired shades, or shades used here as foll:

A	Opaque 112	3 balls
B	Ripple 121	1 ball
C	Fresh 131	1 ball

NEEDLES AND HOOK

Pair of size 2 (3mm) knitting needles
Size C-2 (2.50mm) crochet hook

EXTRAS

Magnetic snap
Cotton lining fabric 14 in./35cm by 28 in./70cm
23½ in./60cm of 1½ in./4cm wide grosgrain ribbon
Matching sewing thread
1¾ yd/150cm of 1½ in./4cm wide satin ribbon

GAUGE

28 sts and 38 rows to 4 in./10cm measured over stockinette stitch using size 2 (3mm) needles.

FRONT AND BACK (BOTH ALIKE)

Using size 2 (3mm) needles and yarn A, cast on 61 sts.
Beg with a K row, work in St st for 2 rows, ending with RS facing for next row.
Row 3 (RS): K2, inc in next st, K to last 4 sts, inc in next st, K3.
Row 4: P2, inc purlwise in next st, P to last 4 sts, inc purlwise in next st, P3. 65 sts.
Working all increases as set by last 2 rows, inc one st at each end of next 3 rows, then on EOR 5 times. 81 sts.
Work even until piece measures

8¾ in./22cm, ending with **WS** facing for next row.

Next row (WS): K to end (to form fold line).

Beg with a K row, work 16 more rows in St st. Bind off.

GUSSET AND HANDLE

Using size 2 (3mm) needles and yarn A, cast on 13 sts.

Beg with a K row, work in St st for 22½ in./57cm, ending with RS facing for next row.

This section forms gusset.

Shape handle

Cast on 7 sts at beg of next 2 rows. 27 sts.

Next row (RS): K7, sl 1, K11, sl 1, K7.

Next row: P to end.

Rep last 2 rows until handle measures 21¼ in./54cm from cast-on sts (43¾ in./111cm in total), ending with RS facing for next row. Bind off.

FLOWER MOTIF

Using size C-2 (2.50mm) crochet hook and yarn C, ch8 and join with a slip st in first ch to form a ring.

Round 1 (RS): Ch1 (does NOT count as st), 16sc in ring, join with a slip st in first sc. Do not turn at end of rounds, but work with RS always facing.

Round 2: Ch12 (counts as 1tr and 8ch), skip first 2sc, (1tr in next sc, ch8, skip 1sc) 7 times, join with a slip st in 4th of 12ch at beg of round.

Round 3: Ch1 (does NOT count as st), (1sc, 1hdc, 1dc, 3tr, ch4, 1 slip st in last tr, 2tr, 1dc, 1hdc, and 1sc) in each ch sp to end, join with a slip st in first sc.
Fasten off.

PAISLEY MOTIF

Note: Paisley motif is for experienced crocheters only. For an easier option,

replace this motif with a second flower motif worked with yarn B.

For the paisley motif, beg as foll:

Using size C-2 (2.50mm) crochet hook and yarn B, ch67.

Row 1 (RS): 2dc in 4th ch from hook (to form first shell), *skip 2ch, (1 slip st, ch3, and 2dc) in next ch (to form shell), rep from * 14 times more, skip 2ch, insert hook in next ch and in ch at base of 2dc at beg of row (taking care not to twist work and keeping foundation ch in front of work), yo and draw loop through both of ch and loop on hook, ch3, then cont working into rem foundation ch only, work 2dc in same place as where hook was last inserted, **skip 2ch, (1 slip st, ch3, and 2dc) in next ch, rep from ** 3 times more, skip 2ch, 1 slip st in last ch. Fasten off.

This forms outline of paisley motif. (21 shells in total—16 forming loop and 5 forming tail.)

Now work flower for center as foll:

Using size C-2 (2.50mm) crochet hook and yarn B, ch8 and join with a slip st in first ch to form a ring.

Round 1 (RS): Ch3, 1dc in ring, (ch4, 1 slip st in 4th ch from hook, 2dc in ring) 8 times, ch4, 1 slip st in 4th ch from hook, join with a slip st in 3rd of 3ch at beg of round, join in 2nd strand of yarn and using yarn DOUBLE ch4 (to form upper part of stem), *using yarn SINGLE ch5, then with RS of outline facing, work 1 slip st in ch at base of 4th shell of outline, ch2, skip (2ch and 1 slip st), 1dc in next ch, 1tr in each of next 2ch, 1dc in next ch, 1 slip st in next ch (to complete leaf), rep from * once more but attaching this leaf to corresponding point along other side of outline (in ch at base of 14th shell of outline), using yarn DOUBLE ch4 (to form lower part of stem), join with a slip st to

point where outline meets.
Fasten off.

Sew ch loops of flower section to inside of outline, leaving loops nearest stem free.

FINISHING

Block then press pieces lightly on WS, following instructions on yarn label.

Using knitted pieces as a guide, cut out lining pieces from fabric—cut out front and back (to fold line row) and gusset section of gusset and handle, adding seam allowance along all edges.

On knitted bag, fold upper edge of front and back to inside along fold line row and stitch in place. Sew together cast-on and bound-off ends of gusset and handle. Fold edges of handle section to inside along slipped st fold lines and sew row-end edges together along handle section. Thread grosgrain ribbon through handle section and secure in place. Matching ends of gusset section to fold line rows of front and back, sew sides of gusset to front and back.

Sew together lining sections in same way as for knitted sections. Fold seam allowance to WS around top edges. Slip lining inside bag and slip stitch folded edges in place. Sew on magnetic snap to close top edges.

Using size C-2 (2.50mm) crochet hook and yarn B throughout, make circles motif as given on pages 118 and 119.

Using photograph as a guide, sew flower, circles, and paisley motifs to front of bag. Lay satin ribbon over gusset and handle and sew in place. Form remaining length of ribbon into a bow and sew to one end of handle as in photograph.

Lace Shawl

Knitted in superlight Rowan Kidsilk Haze in a lacy pattern stitch, this gossamer shawl is the ultimate in dressed-up luxury with a spectacular, ethereal feel. Wear it over an evening gown or summer dress as a mere whisper of a cover-up, to add a touch of magic to your outfit. The ends of the shawl are slipped through a smart knitted beaded loop to keep it in place around your shoulders.

LACE SHAWL by Sharon Miller

FINISHED SIZE
Finished wrap measures 15½ in./39cm wide by 50½ in./128cm long.

YARN
2 balls of Rowan *Kidsilk Haze* (25g/1oz) in desired shade (Smoke 605 was used here)

NEEDLES
Pair of size 6 (4mm) and size 10½ (7mm) knitting needles

EXTRAS
3mm round glass beads, approximately 120, in silver (Rowan no. 01008)
2¼ in./6cm of ½ in./6mm wide elastic

GAUGE
16 sts and 18 rows to 4 in./10cm measured over pattern (after blocking) using size 10½ (7mm) needles.

SPECIAL ABBREVIATION
bead 1 = bring yarn to RS of work, slide bead up next to stitch just worked, slip next stitch purlwise from left needle to right needle and take yarn back to WS of work, leaving bead sitting on RS of work in front of slipped st.

PATTERN NOTE
This shawl uses the knitted cast-on method. To work this cast-on, first make a slip knot on the left needle. Then insert the right needle into the slip knot knitwise. Wrap the yarn around the right needle and pull a loop through the slip knot, leaving the slip knot in place on the left needle. Next, insert the tip of the left needle from right to left through the new loop on the right needle and slip this loop onto the left needle. Continue in this way until there are the required number of cast-on sts on the left needle. This provides the ideal cast-on edge for lace knitting.

TO MAKE SHAWL
Using 10½ (7mm) needles and the knit-on cast-on method, cast on 62 sts. Work in garter st (knit every row) for 2 rows, ending with RS facing for next row.
Row 3 (RS): K1, *yo, K2tog, rep from * to last st, K1.
Row 4: Rep row 3.
Row 5: K1, yo, K2tog, K to last 3 sts, yo, K2tog, K1.
Rows 6 to 10: Rep row 5 five times.
Row 11: K1, yo, K2tog, K10, (yo, K2tog, K15) twice, yo, K2tog, K10, yo, K2tog, K1.
Row 12 and every even-numbered row to row 220: K1, yo, K2tog, K to last 3 sts, yo, K2tog, K1.
Row 13: K1, yo, K2tog, K8, (yo, K2tog, K1, yo, K2tog, K12) twice, yo, K2tog, K1, yo, K2tog, K9, yo, K2tog, K1.
Row 15: K1, yo, K2tog, K6, *(yo, K2tog, K1) twice, yo, K2tog, K9, rep from * once more, (yo, K2tog, K1) twice, yo, K2tog, K8, yo, K2tog, K1.
Row 17: K1, yo, K2tog, K4, *(yo, K2tog, K1) 3 times, yo, K2tog, K6, rep from * twice more, K1, yo, K2tog, K1.
Row 19: K1, yo, K2tog, K2, *(yo, K2tog, K1) 4 times, yo, K2tog, K3, rep from * twice more, K3, yo, K2tog, K1.
Row 21: K1, yo, K2tog, K3, *(yo, K2tog, K1) 4 times, yo, K2tog, K3, rep from * twice more, K2, yo, K2tog, K1.
Row 23: K1, yo, K2tog, K4, *(yo, K2tog, K1) 4 times, yo, K2tog, K3, rep from * twice more, K1, yo, K2tog, K1.
Row 25: K1, yo, K2tog, K5, *(yo, K2tog, K1) 4 times, yo, K2tog, K3, rep from * twice more, yo, K2tog, K1.
Row 27: K1, yo, K2tog, K6, *(yo, K2tog, K1) 4 times, yo, K2tog, K3, rep from * once more, (yo, K2tog, K1) 4 times, yo,

K2tog, K2, yo, K2tog, K1.
Row 29: K1, yo, K2tog, K5, *(K2tog, yo, K1) 4 times, K2tog, yo, K3, rep from * twice more, yo, K2tog, K1.
Row 31: K1, yo, K2tog, K4, *(K2tog, yo, K1) 4 times, K2tog, yo, K3, rep from * twice more, K1, yo, K2tog, K1.
Row 33: K1, yo, K2tog, K3, *(K2tog, yo, K1) 4 times, K2tog, yo, K3, rep from * twice more, K2, yo, K2tog, K1.
Row 35: K1, yo, K2tog, K2, *(K2tog, yo, K1) 4 times, K2tog, yo, K3, rep from * twice more, K3, yo, K2tog, K1.
Row 36: Rep row 12.
Rep rows 21 to 36, 11 times.
Row 213: K1, yo, K2tog, K1, *(K2tog, yo, K1) 4 times, K2tog, yo, K3, rep from * twice more, K4, yo, K2tog, K1.
Row 215: K1, yo, K2tog, K3, *(K2tog, yo, K1) 3 times, K2tog, yo, K6, rep from * twice more, K2, yo, K2tog, K1.
Row 217: K1, yo, K2tog, K5, *(K2tog, yo, K1) twice, K2tog, yo, K9, rep from * twice more, yo, K2tog, K1.
Row 219: K1, yo, K2tog, K7, (K2tog, yo, K1, K2tog, yo, K12) twice, K2tog, yo, K1, K2tog, yo, K10, yo, K2tog, K1.
Row 221: K1, yo, K2tog, K9, (K2tog, yo, K15) twice, K2tog, yo, K11, yo, K2tog, K1.
Rows 222 to 226: Rep row 5, 5 times.
Rows 227 and 228: Rep rows 3 and 4.
Work in garter st for 2 rows, ending with RS facing for next row.
Bind off loosely.

BEADED LOOP
Thread all beads onto yarn before casting on.
Using size 6 (4mm) needles, cast on 25 sts.
Patt row 1 (RS): K1, (bead 1, K1) 12 times.
Patt row 2: Knit.
Patt row 3: K2, (bead 1, K1) 11 times, K1.
Patt row 4: Knit.
These 4 rows form patt.

Work 16 more rows in patt, ending with
RS facing for next row.
Bind off.

FINISHING

Pin out shawl to finished measurements
given, using steel pins spaced about
2¼ in./6cm apart along edge, pulling out
at these points to form shaped edging.
Cover with damp cloths and leave to
dry naturally.
Sew together ends of elastic to form
a loop. Sew cast-on and bound-off ends
of beaded strip together to form a loop.
Sew together row-end edges of beaded
loop, enclosing elastic loop inside.

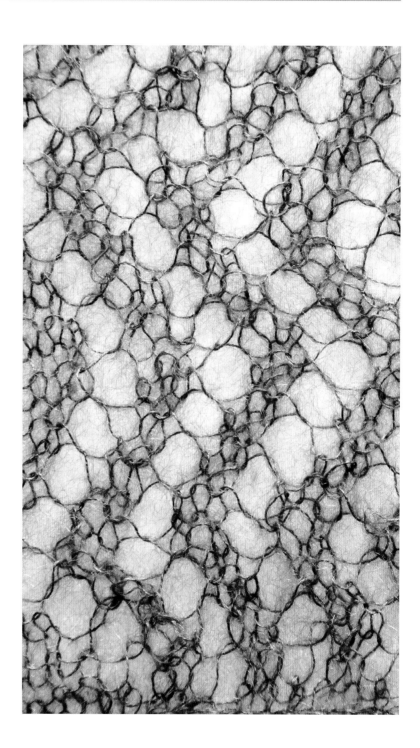

Button Crochet Belt

This is another good project for those new to crochet. Worked in a shiny mercerized cotton, it consists of rows of all the simplest crochet stitches, so making it is good practice in crochet basics. The belt is elaborately edged with a row of buttons. If you wish, add buttons to the ends of the ties, too, for extra embellishment.

BUTTON CROCHET BELT by Jennie Atkinson

FINISHED SIZE

Finished belt measures approximately 24 in./60cm long (excluding ties at each end) by 3³/₄ in./9.5cm wide at center and 2¹/₂ in./6.5cm wide at each end.

YARN

1 ball of Jaeger *Siena* (50g/1³/₄oz) in desired shade (Seaspray 405 was used here)

HOOKS

Sizes B-1 (2.00mm) and D-3 (3.00mm) crochet hooks

EXTRAS

11mm abalone or mother-of-pearl buttons, 80 (Rowan no. 00322 Abalone)

GAUGE

27 sts and 32 rows to 4 in./10cm measured over single crochet using size D-3 (3.00mm) hook.

TO MAKE BELT

Using size D-3 (3.00mm) hook, ch161.

Row 1 (RS): Ch1, 1sc in 2nd ch from hook, 1sc in each of rem 159ch. Turn. 160sc.

Row 2: Ch1, 1sc in each sc to end. Turn.

Row 3: Rep row 2.

Row 4: Ch1, 1sc in each of first 20sc, 1hdc in each of next 20sc, 1dc in each of next 20sc, 1tr in each of next 40sc, 1dc in each of next 20sc, 1hdc in each of next 20sc, 1sc in each of rem 20sc. Turn.

Row 5: Ch1, 1sc in each st to end. Turn.

Rows 6 and 7: Rep row 5 twice.

Row 8: Ch1, 1sc in each of first 18 sts, 1hdc in each of next 18 sts, 1dc in each of next 18 sts, 1tr in each of next 52 sts, 1dc in each of next 18 sts, 1hdc in each of next 18 sts, 1sc in each of rem 18 sts. Turn.

Rows 9, 10, and 11: Rep row 5 three times.

Row 12: Ch1, 1sc in each of first 16 sts, 1hdc in each of next 16 sts, 1dc in each of next 16 sts, 1tr in each of next 64 sts, 1dc in each of next 16 sts, 1hdc in each of next 16 sts, 1sc in each of rem 16 sts. Turn.

Rows 13, 14, and 15: Rep row 5 three times.

Row 16: Ch1, 1sc in each of first 14 sts, 1hdc in each of next 14 sts, 1dc in each of next 14 sts, 1tr in each of next 76 sts, 1dc in each of next 14 sts, 1hdc in each of next 14 sts, 1sc in each of rem 14 sts. Turn.

Rows 17, 18, and 19: Rep row 5 three times.

Fasten off.

FINISHING

Weave in loose ends.

Block then press lightly on WS, following instructions on yarn label.

Ties

Using size B-1 (2.00mm) hook, join yarn with a slip st in one corner of one end of belt and work chain sts until tie is approximately 30 in./75cm long.

Fasten off.

Work a tie in same way at other corner at same end of belt, then a third tie equally spaced between first two.

Knot each of three ties ³/₈ in./1cm from end.

Work three ties at other end of belt in same way.

Weave in all loose ends.

Using yarn, sew 40 buttons along top and 40 buttons along bottom edge of belt as shown.

Crochet Cap

This 30s revival cap would be a stylish finishing touch for any outfit. A row of charming flower motifs is made first and the filet crochet top is worked directly onto them. Make a few in different shades of Rowan's 4-Ply Cotton so you have one for every occasion. Once you get the hang of the structure, you can choose any crochet motif you like and compose your own version of this design.

CROCHET CAP by Kim Hargreaves

SIZE
To fit average size adult head.

YARN
1 x ball of Rowan *4-Ply Cotton* (50g/1³/₄oz) in desired shade (Ripple 121 was used here)

CROCHET HOOK
Size C-2 (2.50mm) crochet hook

GAUGE
One motif measures 3 in./7.5cm square using size C-2 (2.50mm) hook.

SPECIAL ABBREVIATION
ssc (spike single crochet) = insert hook 2 rounds below next st (i.e. through top of round 1), wrap yarn around hook and draw loop through bringing loop up to height of current round, wrap yarn around hook and draw through both loops on hook to complete st.

MOTIF BORDER
First motif
Using size C-2 (2.50mm) hook, ch6 and join with a slip st in first ch to form a ring.
Round 1 (RS): Ch1 (does NOT count as st), 16sc in ring, join with a slip st in first sc. Do not turn at end of rounds, but work with RS always facing. 16sc.
Round 2: Ch1 (does NOT count as st), 1sc in each of first 2sc, *(1sc, ch9, 1sc) all in next sc, 1sc in each of next 3sc, rep from * twice, (1sc, ch9, 1sc) all in next sc, 1sc in last sc, join with a slip st in first sc.
Round 3: Ch1 (does NOT count as st), 1sc in first sc, *skip 2sc, (2hdc, 17dc, 2hdc) all in next ch sp, skip 2sc, 1sc in next sc, rep from * 3 times omitting sc at end of last rep, join

with a slip st in first sc.
Round 4: Ch1 (does NOT count as st), 1ssc over first st, *ch5, skip 5 sts, 1sc in next st, ch3, 1 slip st in 3rd ch from hook, (ch5, skip 4 sts, 1sc in next st, ch3, 1 slip st in 3rd ch from hook) twice, ch5, skip 5 sts, 1ssc over next st, rep from * 3 times more omitting ssc at end of last rep, join with a slip st in first sc.
Fasten off.
Motif forms a square shape, made up of 4 "petals" pointing out toward corners of square. Around each "petal" there are 3 picot loops—one in each corner of square and 2 along sides of square.
Make 5 more motifs in same way, joining them to previous motifs *while working round 4* by replacing appropriate "ch3" of side picot loops with "ch1, 1 slip st in adjacent side picot loop, ch1." Do NOT join motifs at corner picot loops.
Join first 5 motifs to form a strip, joining new motif to previous motif along one side. When working 6th motif, join this motif along two opposite sides to first and 5th motifs to form a loop.

LOWER EDGING
Using size C-2 (2.50mm) hook and with RS facing, rejoin yarn with a slip st in one picot loop along lower edge of motif border and cont as foll:
Round 1 (RS): *Ch5, 1 slip st in next picot loop, rep from * to end, working last slip st in same place as slip st attaching yarn. Do not turn at end of rounds, but work with RS always facing. 24 ch sps.
Round 2: Slip st in first ch sp, ch2 (counts as first hdc), 4hdc in first ch sp, 5hdc in each ch sp to end, join with a slip st in 2nd of 2ch at beg of round. 120 sts.
Fasten off.

CROWN
Using size C-2 (2.50mm) hook and with RS facing, rejoin yarn with a slip st in one picot loop along top edge of motif border and work as for lower edging to end of round 2.
Round 3: Ch4 (counts as 1dc and 1ch), skip first 2 sts, *1dc in next hdc, ch1, skip 1hdc, rep from * to end, join with a slip st in 3rd of 4ch at beg of round. 120 sts, 60 ch sps.
Round 4: Ch4 (counts as 1dc and 1ch), skip first 2 sts, *1dc in next dc, ch1, skip 1ch, rep from * to end, join with a slip st in 3rd of 4ch at beg of round.
Rounds 5 and 6: Rep round 4 twice.
Round 7: Ch4 (counts as 1dc and 1ch), skip first 4 sts, *1dc in next dc, (ch1, skip 1ch, 1dc in next dc) 8 times, ch1, skip 3 sts, rep from * 4 times, 1dc in next dc, (ch1, skip 1ch, 1dc in next dc) 7 times, ch1, skip 1ch, join with a slip st in 3rd of 4ch at beg of round. 108 sts, 54 ch sps.
Round 8: Rep round 4.
Round 9: Ch4 (counts as 1dc and 1ch), skip first 4 sts, *1dc in next dc, (ch1, skip 1ch, 1dc in next dc) 7 times, ch1, skip 3 sts, rep from * 4 times, 1dc in next dc, (ch1, skip 1ch, 1dc in next dc) 6 times, ch1, skip 1ch, join with a slip st in 3rd of 4ch at beg of round. 96 sts, 48 ch sps.
Round 10: Rep round 4.
Round 11: Ch4 (counts as 1dc and 1ch), skip first 4 sts, *1dc in next dc, (ch1, skip 1ch, 1dc in next dc) 6 times, ch1, skip 3 sts, rep from * 4 times, 1dc in next dc, (ch1, skip 1ch, 1dc in next dc) 5 times, ch1, skip 1ch, join with a slip st in 3rd of 4ch at beg of round. 84 sts, 42 ch sps.
Round 12: Ch4 (counts as 1dc and 1ch), skip first 4 sts, *1dc in next dc, (ch1, skip

1ch, 1dc in next dc) 5 times, ch1, skip
3 sts, rep from * 4 times, 1dc in next dc,
(ch1, skip 1ch, 1dc in next dc) 4 times,
ch1, skip 1ch, join with a slip st in 3rd of
4ch at beg of round.
72 sts, 36 ch sps.
Round 13: Ch4 (counts as 1dc and 1ch),
skip first 4 sts, *1dc in next dc, (ch1, skip
1ch, 1dc in next dc) 4 times, ch1, skip
3 sts, rep from * 4 times, 1dc in next dc,
(ch1, skip 1ch, 1dc in next dc) 3 times,
ch1, skip 1ch, join with a slip st in 3rd of
4ch at beg of round. 60 sts, 30 ch sps.
Round 14: Ch4 (counts as 1dc and 1ch),
skip first 4 sts, *1dc in next dc, (ch1, skip
1ch, 1dc in next dc) 3 times, ch1, skip
3 sts, rep from * 4 times, 1dc in next dc,
(ch1, skip 1ch, 1dc in next dc) twice, ch1,
skip 1ch, join with a slip st in 3rd of 4ch
at beg of round. 48 sts, 24 ch sps.
Round 15: Ch4 (counts as 1dc and 1ch),
skip first 4 sts, *1dc in next dc, ch1, skip
(1ch, 1dc and 1ch), rep from * 10 times,
join with a slip st in 3rd of 4ch at beg of
round. 24 sts, 12 ch sps.
Round 16: Ch4 (counts as 1dc and 1ch),
skip first 4 sts, *1dc in next dc, ch1, skip
(1ch, 1dc and 1ch), rep from * 4 times,
join with a slip st in 3rd of 4ch at beg of
round. 12 sts, 6 ch sps.
Fasten off.

FINISHING
Weave in loose ends.
Block then press lightly on WS, following
instructions on yarn label.

Buttoned Bag

Simple but sophisticated, this will tempt first-time knitters to practice their skills. Worked in Rowan Scottish Tweed DK in simple stockinette stitch, with garter stitch handles, it couldn't be easier to knit. Adding the buttons and beads is a little more time consuming, but worth every minute of effort!

BUTTONED BAG by KIM HARGREAVES

FINISHED SIZE
Finished bag measures approximately
9½ in./24cm wide by 10¾ in./27cm tall.

YARN
2 balls of Rowan *Scottish Tweed DK*
(50g/1¾oz) in desired shade (Grey Mist
001 was used here)

NEEDLES
Pair each of size 3 (3.25mm) and size 6
(4mm) knitting needles

EXTRAS
14mm dark mother-of-pearl buttons,
12 (Rowan no. 00321 Shell)
11mm dark mother-of-pearl buttons,
126 (Rowan no. 00320 Shell)
3mm round glass beads, 276, in pewter
(Rowan no. 01006)
Lining fabric 12 in./30cm by 28 in./70cm
and matching sewing thread

GAUGE
21 sts and 29 rows to 4 in./10cm measured
over St st using size 6 (4mm) needles.

FRONT
Using size 6 (4mm) needles, cast on
50 sts.
Beg with a K row, work in St st until front
measures 10¾ in./27cm from cast-on
edge, ending with RS facing for next row.
Bind off.

BACK
Make exactly as for front.

HANDLES (MAKE 2)
Using size 3 (3.25mm) needles, cast on
75 sts.
Work in garter st (knit every row) for
6 rows. Bind off.

FINISHING
Block then press front and back lightly on
WS, following instructions on yarn label.
Do NOT press handles.
Using backstitch, sew front and back
together along both side and lower
(cast-on) edges.
Position handles 2 in./5cm in from side
seams and sew in place inside bag.
Set aside 30 of smaller buttons—these
will be used for the handles. Sew
remaining buttons to front and back of
bag, scattering them evenly as in
photograph. To attach each button, bring
needle up through one hole of the
button, thread two beads onto thread
and then take needle back through other
hole of button, leaving the beads sitting
in the center of the button.
Sew remaining buttons to handles in
same way, positioning 15 buttons evenly
along each handle.
For a lining, cut two pieces of fabric
same size as bag plus ½ in./1.5cm extra
all around each piece for seam
allowance. Sew pieces together along
three sides, then fold ½ in./1.5cm to
wrong side around top edge.
Insert lining inside knitted bag and slip
stitch in place around top.

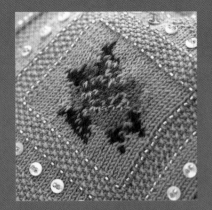 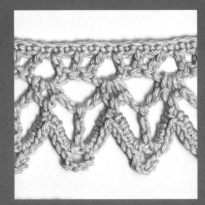 

Techniques

Read this chapter if you need a few helpful
tips to fill in the gaps in your knitting and
crochet skills. There are instructions for how
to crochet in rounds, follow your knitting or
crochet pattern, thread beads, and more.
Knitters who want to experiment with
crochet will also find six very simple crochet
edgings and some more challenging motifs.

WORKING CROCHET IN ROUNDS

The crochet motifs like those used for the Crochet Shawl (see right and pages 88–91) and the Crochet Motif Bag (see pages 92–95) are worked in the round. Each motif is begun at the center and worked outward.

The foundation for the first round of stitches is a chain circle, which is created from a suitable length of foundation chains that are linked end to end to form a ring. Once you have mastered this simple crochet technique, you will find that working crochet in the round is just as easy as working back and forth in rows.

Follow the steps here to practice making the crochet ring and working the first round of stitches into the ring. Then try making the basic crochet motif for the Crochet Shawl. You'll soon have enough confidence to tackle the motifs on pages 116–119.

1 Make a foundation chain of six chains (or the number given in your pattern). Insert the hook into the first chain worked and catch the yarn with hook.

2 Draw the yarn through both the chain and the loop on the hook to join the length of chains into a circle—this is called "join with a slip stitch."

3 The first "round" of the crochet is worked into the ring. The instructions in your pattern for "round 1" will tell you what stitches and how many to work— here single crochet stitches are being worked into the ring. In the following rounds stitches are increased by working twice or more into the same stitch where instructed. The work is not turned at the end of rounds, so the right side of the crochet is always facing you.

1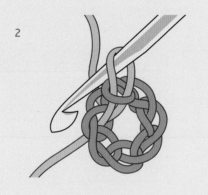

2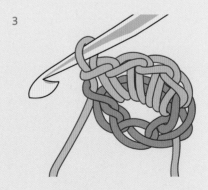

3

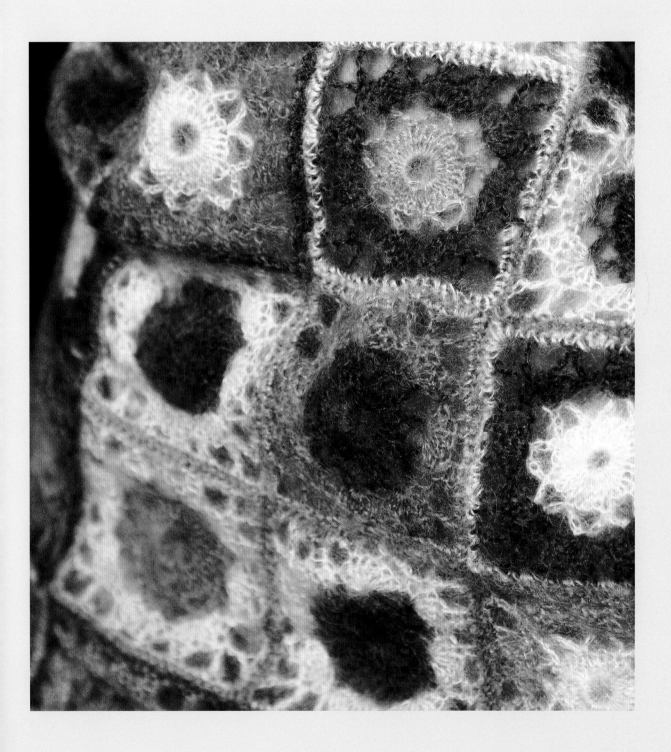

CROCHET MOTIFS

Use these four crochet motifs as decorative items in their own right or as alternatives to the motifs used on the Crochet Motif Bag (see pages 92–95).

The yarns and buttons and beads listed below for the motifs are just suggestions. Experiment with your own combinations to personalize the designs.

FINISHED SIZES

Finished Beaded Square Motif measures 4½ in./11cm square; Button-Trimmed Circle Motif measures 4¾ in./12cm in diameter; Pentagon Motif measures 6 in./15cm at widest point and 4½ in./11cm along each side; and Circles Motif measures 5½ in./14cm in diameter.

YARN

Rowan *Lurex Shimmer*, *Kidsilk Haze*, *4-Ply Soft*, and *4-Ply Cotton* in desired shades, or in shades used here as foll:

Beaded Square Motif

A	*Kidsilk Haze*	Pearl	590
B	*4-Ply Soft*	Day Dream	378
C	*4-Ply Soft*	Irish Cream	386
D	*Kidsilk Haze*	Majestic	589

Button-Trimmed Circle Motif

A	*4-Ply Cotton*	Opaque	112
B	*4-Ply Soft*	Irish Cream	386

Pentagon Motif

A	*Kidsilk Haze*	Pearl	590
B	*Kidsilk Haze*	Majestic	589

Circles Motif

A	*Lurex Shimmer*	Gleam	336
B	*Kidsilk Haze*	Majestic	589
C	*4-Ply Soft*	Day Dream	378
D	*4-Ply Soft*	Irish Cream	386
E	*Kidsilk Haze*	Pearl	590

CROCHET HOOK

Size C-2 (2.50mm) crochet hook

GAUGE

Working to an exact gauge is not essential for these motifs.

EXTRAS

Beaded Square Motif: 3mm round glass beads, 20, in pewter (Rowan no. 01006); 3mm round glass beads, 40, in silver (Rowan no. 01008); 2mm glass beads, 320, in pink (Rowan no. 01019); and matching sewing thread.

Button-trimmed Circle Motif: 17 assorted mother-of-pearl buttons and matching sewing thread.

Circles Motif: 3mm round glass beads, 16, in pewter (Rowan no. 01006); 3mm round glass beads, 24, in silver (Rowan no. 01008); and matching sewing thread.

SPECIAL ABBREVIATIONS

tr3tog = *(yo) twice and insert hook as indicated, yo and draw loop through, (yo and draw through 2 loops) twice, rep from * twice more, yo and draw through all 4 loops on hook.

dc2tog = *yo and insert hook as indicated, yo and draw loop through, yo and draw through 2 loops, rep from * once more, yo and draw through all 3 loops on hook.

dtr3tog = *(yo) 3 times and insert hook as indicated, yo and draw loop through, (yo and draw through 2 loops) 3 times, rep from * twice more, yo and draw through all 4 loops on hook.

dtr4tog = *(yo) 3 times and insert hook as indicated, yo and draw loop through, (yo and draw through 2 loops) 3 times, rep from * 3 times more, yo and draw through all 5 loops on hook.

BEADED SQUARE MOTIF

Using size C-2 (2.50mm) crochet hook and yarn A, ch12 and join with a slip st in first ch to form a ring.

Round 1 (RS): Using yarn A, ch1 (does NOT count as st), 24sc in ring, join with a slip st in first sc. Do not turn at end of rounds, but work with RS always facing.

Round 2: Using yarn A, ch6, skip first sc, dtr3tog over next 3sc, (ch7, dtr4tog over sc just used and next 3sc) 7 times, ch7, join with a slip st in top of dtr3tog. Break off yarn A and join in yarn B.

Round 3: Using yarn B, ch1 (does NOT count as st), 1sc in same place as slip st at end of previous round, *(ch3, skip 1ch, 1sc in next ch) 3 times, ch3, skip 1ch**, 1sc in next dtr4tog, rep from * to end, ending last rep at **, join with a slip st in first sc.

Round 4: Using yarn B, slip st across and in center of first ch sp, ch1 (does NOT count as st), 1sc in first ch sp, *ch3, 1sc in next ch sp, rep from * to end, replacing sc at end of last rep with 1 slip st in first sc.

Round 5: Rep round 4.
Break off yarn B and join in yarn C.

Round 6: Using yarn C, slip st across and in center of first ch sp, ch1 (does NOT count as st), 1sc in first ch sp, *(ch3, 1sc in next ch sp) 4 times, ch3, skip next ch sp, (tr3tog, ch5, dtr4tog, ch4, slip st to top of dtr4tog, ch5, and tr3tog) in next ch sp, ch3, skip next ch sp, 1sc in next ch sp, rep from * to end, replacing sc at end of last rep with 1 slip st in first sc.
Fasten off.

With RS facing and using C-2 (2.50mm) crochet hook, attach yarn D to top of round 2 between 2sc of round 3 and, working in ch sps between sc of round 3, cont as foll:

Next round: Using yarn D, ch1 (does NOT count as st), 1sc in sp where yarn was attached, *ch3, 1sc in next ch sp, rep

Circles Motif (above left) and Beaded Square Motif (above right)

from * to end, replacing sc at end of last rep with 1 slip st in first sc.

Next round: Using yarn D, slip st across and in center of first ch sp, ch1 (does NOT count as st), 1sc in first ch sp, *ch3, 1sc in next ch sp, rep from * to end, replacing sc at end of last rep with 1 slip st in first sc.

Fasten off.

Using photograph as a guide, sew on beads as foll: Sew 8 pewter beads evenly around foundation ch edge. Thread 16 pink beads onto sewing thread and sew ends of this loop of beads to each side of each pewter bead. In same way, sew 3 pewter beads to base of sts at corners of round 6, then sew loops of 16 pink beads to each side of these beads. Sew silver beads to top of each dtr4tog of round 2, gathering up last 2 rounds worked in yarn D. Sew a silver bead to each corner of round 6, then sew on 7 more silver beads along each side.

BUTTON-TRIMMED CIRCLE MOTIF

Using C-2 (2.50mm) crochet hook and yarn A, ch10 and join with a slip st in first ch to form a ring.

Round 1 (RS): Using yarn A, ch6 (counts as first tr and 2ch), (1tr in ring, ch2) 10 times, join with a slip st in 4th of 6ch at beg of round. Do not turn at end of rounds, but work with RS always facing. Break off yarn A and join in yarn B.

Round 2: Using yarn B, ch4 (counts as first tr), 4tr in first ch sp, (1tr in next tr, 3tr in next ch sp) 10 times, join with a slip st in 4th of 4ch at beg of round. 45 sts.

Break off yarn B and join in yarn A.

Round 3: Using yarn A, ch9 (counts as first tr and 5ch), skip first 3 sts, (1tr in next tr, ch5, skip 2tr) 14 times, join with a slip st in 4th of 9ch at beg of

round. 15 ch sps.

Break off yarn A and join in yarn B.

Round 4: Using yarn B, ch4 (counts as first tr), *1tr in each of next 5ch, 1tr in next tr, rep from * to end, replacing tr at end of last rep with 1 slip st in 4th of 4ch at beg of round. 90 sts.

Break off yarn B and join in yarn A.

Round 5: Using yarn A, ch12 (counts as first tr and 8ch), skip first 6 sts, (1tr in next tr, ch8, skip 5tr) 14 times, join with a slip st in 4th of 12ch at beg of round. 15 ch sps.

Fasten off.

Sew assorted buttons at random to rounds 2 and 4.

PENTAGON MOTIF

Using C-2 (2.50mm) crochet hook and yarn A, ch5 and join with a slip st in first ch to form a ring.

Round 1 (RS): Using yarn A, (ch6, 1sc in ring) 5 times. Do not turn at end of rounds, but work with RS always facing. Join in yarn B.

Round 2: Using yarn B, (ch6, 3sc in next ch sp) 5 times.

Round 3: Using yarn A, (ch6, 3sc in next ch sp, 1sc in each of next 2sc, skip 1sc) 5 times.

Round 4: Using yarn B, (ch6, 3sc in next ch sp, 1sc in each of next 4sc, skip 1sc) 5 times.

Round 5: Using yarn A, (ch6, 3sc in next ch sp, 1sc in each of next 6sc, skip 1sc) 5 times.

Round 6: Using yarn B, (ch6, 3sc in next ch sp, 1sc in each of next 8sc, skip 1sc) 5 times.

Round 7: Using yarn A, (ch6, 3sc in next ch sp, 1sc in each of next 10sc, skip 1sc) 5 times.

Round 8: Using yarn B, (ch5, 1sc in next ch sp, ch5, skip 1sc, 1sc in each of next

11sc, skip 1sc) 5 times.

Round 9: Using yarn A, *(ch5, 1sc in next ch sp) twice, ch5, skip 1sc, 1sc in each of next 9sc, skip 1sc, rep from * 4 times.

Round 10: Using yarn B, *(ch5, 1sc in next ch sp) 3 times, ch5, skip 1sc, 1sc in each of next 7sc, skip 1sc, rep from * 4 times.

Round 11: Using yarn A, *(ch5, 1sc in next ch sp) 4 times, ch5, skip 1sc, 1sc in each of next 5sc, skip 1sc, rep from * 4 times.

Round 12: Using yarn B, *(ch5, 1sc in next ch sp) 5 times, ch5, skip 1sc, 1sc in each of next 3sc, skip 1sc, rep from * 4 times.

Break off yarn B.

Round 13: Using yarn A, ch3, 1sc in next ch sp, *(ch3, 1sc in next ch sp) 5 times, ch3, skip 1sc, 1dc in next sc, skip 1sc, ch3, 1sc in next ch sp, rep from * 4 times, replacing sc at end of last rep with 1 slip st in first sc.

Fasten off.

CIRCLES MOTIF

Using C-2 (2.50mm) crochet hook and yarn A, ch8 and join with a slip st in first ch to form a ring.

Round 1 (RS): Using yarn A, ch3 (counts as first dc), 31dc in ring, slip st to top of 3ch at beg of round. Do not turn at end of rounds, but work with RS always facing.

Break off yarn A and join in yarn B.

Round 2: Using yarn B, ch3, (1dc, ch3, and dc2tog) in base of 3ch, *ch7, skip 3dc, (dc2tog, ch3, and dc2tog) in next dc, rep from * 6 times, ch7, skip 3dc, join with a slip st in top of dc at beg of round.

Break off yarn B and join in yarn C.

Round 3: Using yarn C, slip st in first ch sp, ch3, (1dc, ch3, and dc2tog) in same ch sp, *ch7, skip 1ch sp, (dc2tog, ch3, and dc2tog) in next ch sp, rep from * 6 times, ch7, join with a slip st in top of dc at beg of round.

Break off yarn C and join in yarn D.

Round 4: Using yarn D, slip st in first ch sp, ch3, (1dc, ch3, and dc2tog) in same ch sp, *ch4, 1sc in next ch sp of round 2 enclosing ch sp of round 3, ch4,** (dc2tog, ch3, and dc2tog) in next ch sp, rep from * to end, ending last rep at **, join with a slip st in top of dc at beg of round.

Break off yarn D and join in yarn E.

Round 5: Using yarn E, slip st in first ch sp, ch3, (1dc, ch3, and dc2tog) in same ch sp, *ch15, slip st to 12th ch from hook (to form ring), ch3, slip st to top of last dc2tog, 6dc in ring, slip st to next sc of round 4, 8dc in ring,** (dc2tog, ch3, and dc2tog) in next 3ch sp of round 4, rep from * to end, ending last rep at **, join with a slip st in top of dc at beg of round.

Round 6: Using yarn E, *ch1, (dc2tog, ch6, slip st to 5th ch from hook, ch1, and dc2tog) in first ch sp, ch1, slip st to top of next dc2tog, 16dc in ring, slip st to top of next dc2tog, rep from * to end.

Fasten off.

Using photograph as a guide, sew on beads as foll: Sew on a pewter bead between each pair of dc2tog of round 3, then another pewter bead to top of each sc of round 4. Sew on a silver bead between tops of each pair of dc2tog of rounds 4, 5, and 6.

Button-Trimmed Circle Motif (above left) and Pentagon Motif (above right)

SIMPLE CROCHET EDGINGS

You can use these edgings to decorate the plain hanger cover on pages 68–71 or for pillows, towels, cushions, collars, or cuffs. Work them in fine crochet threads or in a lightweight cotton yarn, trying out different hook sizes to suit them.

All these edgings are made on a foundation chain slightly longer than the desired length of the edging, except for the Fan Edging. If you like, you can make a sample swatch of your edging first to work out precisely how many chain stitches to start with.

After finishing an edging, pin it out and press it lightly, then stitch it to the crocheted, knitted, or fabric item it was made for.

TO MAKE LOOP EDGING

To begin, make a foundation chain slightly longer than the desired length of the edging. The number of chains must be a multiple of 4, plus 2 extra.

Row 1 (WS): 1sc in 2nd ch from hook, 1sc in each of rem ch. Turn.

Row 2 (RS): Ch3, skip first 2sc, 1dc in next sc, ch5, *1dc in same sc as last dc, (skip next sc, 1dc in next sc) twice, ch5, rep from * to last 2sc, 1dc in same sc as last dc, skip next sc, 1dc in last sc.
Fasten off.

TO MAKE SCALLOP EDGING

To begin, make a foundation chain slightly longer than the desired length of the edging. The number of chains must be a multiple of 6, plus 2 extra.

Row 1 (WS): 1sc in 2nd ch from hook, 1sc in each of rem ch. Turn.

Row 2 (RS): Ch1, 1sc in first sc, *skip next 2sc, 7tr in next sc, skip next 2sc, 1sc in next sc, rep from * to end.
Fasten off.

TO MAKE CLUSTER EDGING

To begin, make a foundation chain slightly longer than the desired length of the edging. The number of chains must be a multiple of 6, plus 2 extra.

Row 1 (WS): 1sc in 2nd ch from hook, 1sc in each of rem ch. Turn.

Row 2 (RS): Ch4, then leaving last loop of each tr on hook, work 2tr in first sc, yo and draw a loop through all 3 loops on hook (2tr-cluster made), *ch8, 1sc in 3rd ch from hook (picot made), ch5, then leaving last loop of each tr on hook, work 3tr in same sc as last cluster, yo and draw a loop through all 4 loops on hook (3tr-cluster made), skip next 5sc, 3tr-cluster in next sc, rep from * to end, omitting 3tr-cluster at end of last rep.
Fasten off.

TO MAKE FAN EDGING

To begin, ch12.

Row 1 (WS): 1sc in 8th ch from hook, ch5, skip next 3ch, work (1dc, ch3, 1dc) all in next ch. Turn.

Row 2 (RS): Ch3, 9dc in 3ch sp, 1sc in 5ch loop, ch5, 1sc in 7ch loop at end. Turn.

Row 3: Ch7, 1sc in 5ch loop, ch5, work (1dc, ch3, 1dc) all in 5th dc (center dc) of 9dc group. Turn.

Rep rows 2 and 3 until edging is desired length, ending with a row 2.
Fasten off.

TO MAKE VENETIAN EDGING

To begin, make a foundation chain slightly longer than the desired length of the edging. The number of chains must be a multiple of 5, plus 2 extra.

Row 1 (WS): 1sc in 2nd ch from hook, 1sc in each of rem ch. Turn.

Row 2 (RS): Ch6, 1dc in first sc, *(skip next sc, 1dc in next sc) twice, ch3, 1dc in next sc, rep from * to end. Turn.

Row 3: Ch1, work (1sc, ch3, 1sc) all in first 3ch sp, *ch5, work (1sc, ch3, 1sc) all in next 3ch sp, rep from *, working last (1sc, ch3, 1sc) all in 6ch loop at end. Turn.

Row 4: Ch1, 1sc in first 3ch loop, *ch4, 1tr in next 5ch loop, ch4, 1sc in next 3ch loop, rep from * to end. Turn.

Row 5: 5sc in first 4ch loop, *ch5, 5sc in each of next 2 4ch loops, rep from *, ending with ch5, 5sc in last 4ch loop.
Fasten off.

TO MAKE DOUBLE-PICOT EDGING

To begin, make a foundation chain slightly longer than the desired length of the edging. The number of chains must be a multiple of 7, plus 6 extra.

Row 1 (RS): 1sc in 2nd ch from hook, 1sc in each of next 2ch, *ch4 and work 1sc in 4th ch from hook—called *make picot*—, 1sc in each of next 2ch, turn, ch9, 1sc in 3rd sc before picot, turn, work (5sc, make picot, 3sc, make picot, 5sc) all in 9ch loop, 1sc in each of next 5ch, rep from * to end, omitting 5sc at end of last rep.
Fasten off.

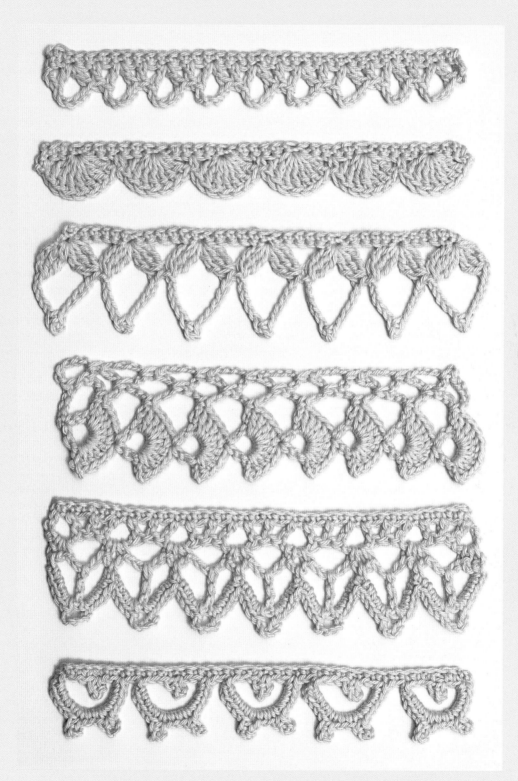

Right from top to bottom:
Loop edging, Scallop Edging,
Cluster edging, Fan Edging,
Venetian Edging, and
Double-Picot Edging

FOLLOWING KNITTING AND CROCHET PATTERNS

The following tips will help you understand the knitting and crochet patterns in this book.

READING A PATTERN

Read the instructions from start to finish before beginning to knit or crochet. You will not necessarily understand everything until you are in the process of working the item, but it will give you an idea of the skill level required for the pattern.

The size of the garment or accessory is given first in the pattern. Where more than one size is given for a garment, instructions for the smallest size comes first, with the larger sizes following it in brackets. If only one figure is given, it applies to all sizes. Where a 0 (zero) or hyphen appears instead of a number, this means that these instructions do not apply to that particular size. Choose your size before beginning (see below) and stick to the same size throughout.

Knit or crochet all the pieces in the order given in the pattern. For the abbreviations used in the patterns, see page 125. (Yarn information is given on pages 126 and 127.)

GAUGE

Pay particular attention to the gauge given in the pattern. Obtaining the correct gauge can make the difference between a successfully knitted or crocheted piece or a disastrous one. Any variation from the quoted gauge, however slight, can distort the size and shape of your finished knitting or crochet.

The correct gauge is given at the start of each pattern. You must match this in order to make your garment or accessory to the recommended size and shape. Because not everyone knits or crochets using the same tension on the

yarn, make a test swatch to see if you need to use a larger or smaller knitting needle or crochet hook size to achieve the specified gauge.

Using the stated knitting needle or crochet hook size and the correct yarn, knit or crochet a square in pattern and/or stockinette stitch (depending on the pattern instructions) of perhaps 5–10 more stitches and 5–10 more rows than those given in the gauge note. Then block and press the finished square lightly as recommended on the yarn label and mark out the central 4 in./10cm square with pins. If you have too many stitches to 4 in./10cm, try again using larger knitting needles or a larger crochet hook. If you have too few stitches to 4 in./10cm, try again using smaller needles or hook. Once you have achieved the correct gauge, your garment or accessory will be worked to the measurements indicated in the pattern instructions.

CHOOSING AND ADJUSTING A GARMENT SIZE

Included with each garment pattern is a size diagram of the finished garment and its dimensions. This diagram shows the finished width of the garment at the underarm point, and when choosing which size to knit or crochet, it is this measurement that the knitter decides on first. A useful tip is to measure one of your own garments that is a comfortable fit.

Having chosen a size based on width, look at the corresponding length for that size. If you are not happy with the total recommended length, you can usually adjust the length of the garment before beginning the armhole shaping. Any adjustment after this point will mean that your sleeve will not properly fit into

the armhole. Don't forget to take your adjustment into account if there is any side seam shaping.

Finally, look at the sleeve length. The size diagram shows the finished sleeve measurement, taking into account any top-arm insertion length. Measure your body between the center of your neck and your wrist, this measurement should correspond to half the garment width plus the sleeve length. Again, the sleeve length can usually be adjusted, but remember to take into consideration the sleeve increases if you do adjust the length. You must increase more frequently than the pattern states to shorten your sleeve, less frequently to lengthen it.

FOLLOWING KNITTING CHARTS

A few of the knitting patterns in this book are worked from charts. Each square on a chart represents a stitch and each line of squares a row of knitting. Symbols or colors are used to represent yarn colors, beads, or stitches. Look at the key with each chart to understand the symbols and colors.

Unless stated otherwise, when working from charts, read odd-numbered rows (knit rows) from right to left and even rows (purl rows) from left to right.

KNITTING WITH COLOR

There are two main methods of working color into a knitted fabric—intarsia and Fair Isle techniques. The first method produces a single thickness of fabric and is usually used where a color is only required in a particular area of a row and does not form a repeating pattern across the row, as in the Fair Isle technique.

Intarsia knitting: The simplest way to work intarsia knitting is to cut short

lengths of yarn for each motif or block of color used in a row. Then joining in the various colors at the appropriate point on the row, link one color to the next by twisting them around each other where they meet on the wrong side to avoid gaps forming in the textile. All loose ends can then either be darned in when the item is completed or can be woven into the back of the work in much the same way as yarns are woven in when working the Fair Isle technique.

Fair Isle knitting: When two or three colors are worked repeatedly across a row, strand the yarn not in use loosely behind the stitches being worked. If you are working with more than two colors, treat the "floating" yarns as if they were one yarn and always spread the stitches to their correct width to keep them elastic. It is advisable not to carry the stranded or "floating" yarns over more than three stitches at a time; instead weave them under and over the color you are working with to catch them into the back of the knitting.

CROCHET TIPS

See the crochet abbreviations and terms on page 125. There are also instructions for working crochet in rounds on page 114.

WORKING WITH BEADS

When beads are worked into the knitted or crocheted fabric, as in some of the designs in this book, you must thread the beads onto the yarn before you start the project.

To do this, fold a length of sewing thread in half and thread both ends through a fine sewing needle—one that will pass easily through the beads. Pass the end of the yarn through this loop of sewing thread. Then thread a bead onto the sewing thread and gently slide it along and onto knitting yarn (see below). Continue in this way until the required number of beads are on the yarn.

FINISHING INSTRUCTIONS

After working for hours on your knitting or crochet, be sure to block and finish the work carefully. The following tips will give you a truly professional-looking result.

BLOCKING AND PRESSING

Darn in all ends neatly along the selvage edge or a color join, as appropriate.

Block out each piece of knitting or crochet facedown, using pins. Then gently press each piece with steam, holding a steam iron just above the surface. Avoid steaming ribbing or any other raised textured areas, and carefully follow the instructions on the yarn label for ironing recommendations. Take special care to press the edges, as this will make sewing the seams both easier and neater.

STITCHING SEAMS

When stitching the pieces together, remember to match areas of color and texture very carefully where they meet. Use a seam stitch such as backstitch or mattress stitch for all main knitting seams and join all ribbing and neckband with a flat seam, unless otherwise stated. For crochet, use backstitch unless stated otherwise.

The pattern instructions specify which seams to work first and which to work last. On garments the shoulder seams are usually joined first. Then the sleeves are sewn to the body, so that the center of the top of the sleeve is aligned with the shoulder seam. Join side and sleeve seams before or after the sleeves are set in depending on your pattern instructions.

FINISHING TOUCHES

When all the seams have been completed on your knitting or crochet, sew on any buttons to correspond with buttonholes, using a matching sewing thread. Then press the seams and any hems, avoiding ribbing or any other raised texture areas of the knitting or crochet.

ABBREVIATIONS AND GLOSSARY

The abbreviations used in this book are given below. Any special abbreviations specific to a pattern are given within the pattern.

KNITTING ABBREVIATIONS

alt	alternate
beg	begin(ning)
cm	centimeter(s)
cont	continu(e)(ing)
dec	decreas(e)(ing)
EOR	every other row
foll	follow(s)(ing)
g	gram(s)
in	inch(es)
inc	increase(e)(ing); or increase one st by working into front and back of stitch
K	knit
K2tog	knit next 2 sts together
m	meter(s)
M1	make one st by picking up strand between st just knit and next st with tip of left needle and working into back of it
mm	millimeter(s)
oz	ounce(s)
P	purl
P2tog	purl next 2 sts together
patt	pattern; or work in pattern
psso	pass slipped stitch over
rem	remain(s)(ing)
rep	repeat(s)(ing)
rev St st	reverse stockinette stitch
RS	right side
sl	slip
skp	slip 1, K1, psso
st(s)	stitch(es)
St st	stockinette stitch
tbl	through back of loop(s)
tog	together
WS	wrong side
yd	yard(s)
yo	yarn over (yarn around right needle to make an extra stitch)

* Repeat instructions after asterisk or between asterisks as many times as instructed.

US AND UK KNITTING TERMINOLOGY

The knitting patterns in this book use US knitting terminology. Some knitting terms are different in the UK.

US equivalent	UK terminology
bind off	cast off
moss stitch	seed stitch
stockinette stitch	stocking stitch
gauge	tension (size of stitch)
work even	work straight
yarn over (yo)	yfrn, yfwd, yon, yrn

CROCHET ABBREVIATIONS AND TERMS

Some basic crochet stitches have different names in the US and UK. The crochet patterns in this book use US terminology. The UK equivalents for US terms are given below. See Knitting Abbreviations for other general abbreviations also used for crochet.

US terminology	UK equivalent
ch chain	**ch** chain
sc single crochet	**dc** double crochet
tr treble	**dtr** double treble
hdc half double	**htr** half treble
skip	**miss**
slip st slip stitch	**ss** slip stitch
sp(s) space(s)	**sp(s)** space(s)
dc double crochet	**tr** treble
dtr double treble	**trtr** triple treble
yo yarn over hook	**yoh** yarn over hook

YARN INFORMATION

Yarn colors are changed regularly by yarn manufacturers, so it is not possible to guarantee that all the shades quoted in this book will still be on sale when you use this book. Although the shades used for each design are given within the pattern instructions, feel free to make your own choice of colors to suit your wardrobe or interior.

It is best to use the specific brand and type of yarn recommended in the pattern whenever possible. If, however, you need to use a substitute, buy yarn by figuring out how many yards/meters you need rather than how much in weight.

The Rowan and Jaeger yarns used in this book are listed here to help you find a comparable substitute if necessary. The specified gauge and knitting-needle size will help you find a yarn of similar thickness.

ROWAN YARNS USED IN THIS BOOK

2 ROWAN COTTON GLACE
- A lightweight cotton yarn; 100 percent cotton
- 50g/1¾oz (approximately 126yd/115m) per ball
- Recommended gauge: 23 sts and 32 rows to 4 in./10cm measured over St st using sizes 3–5 (3.25–3.75mm) knitting needles

1 ROWAN 4-PLY COTTON
- A lightweight cotton yarn; 100 percent cotton
- 50g/1¾oz (approximately 186yd/170m) per ball
- Recommended gauge: 27–29 sts and 37–39 rows to 4 in./10cm measured over St st using sizes 2–3 (3–3.25mm) knitting needles

1 ROWAN 4-PLY SOFT
- A lightweight wool yarn; 100 percent merino wool
- 50g/1¾oz (aproximately 191yd/175m) per ball
- Recommended gauge: 28 sts and 36 rows to 4 in./10cm measured over St st using size 3 (3.25mm) knitting needles

4 ROWAN KID CLASSIC
- A medium-weight mohair-mix yarn; 70 percent lambswool, 26 percent kid mohair, and 4 percent nylon
- 50g/1¾oz (approximately 153yd/140m) per ball
- Recommended gauge: 18–19 sts and 23–25 rows to 4 in./10cm measured over St st using sizes 8–9 (5–5.5mm) knitting needles

2 ROWAN KIDSILK HAZE
- A fine mohair yarn; 70 percent super kid mohair and 30 percent silk
- 25g/1oz (approximately 229yd/210m) per ball
- Recommended gauge: 18–25 sts and 23–34 rows to 4 in./10cm over St st using sizes 3–8 (3.25–5mm) knitting needles

1 ROWAN LUREX SHIMMER
- A fine metallic yarn; 80 percent viscose and 20 percent polyester
- 1oz/25g (approximately 104yd/95m) per ball
- Recommended gauge: 29 sts and 41 rows to 4 in./10cm over St st using size 3 (3.25mm) knitting needles

3 ROWAN RYC BABY CASHSOFT DK
- A medium-weight wool-and-cashmere-mix yarn; 57 percent extra fine merino wool, 33 percent microfiber, and 10 percent cashmere

- 50g/1¾oz (approximately 142yd/130m) per ball
- Recommended gauge: 22 sts and 30 rows to 4 in./10cm measured over St st using size 6 (4mm) knitting needles

1 ROWAN RYC CASHSOFT 4-PLY
- A lightweight wool-and-cashmere-mix yarn; 57 percent extra fine merino wool, 33 percent microfiber, and 10 percent cashmere
- 50g/1¾oz (approximately 197yd/180m) per ball
- Recommended gauge: 28 sts and 36 rows to 4 in./10cm measured over St st using size 3 (3.25mm) knitting needles

JAEGER YARNS USED IN THIS BOOK

1 JAEGER SIENA
- A lightweight cotton yarn; 100 percent mercerized cotton
- 50g/1¾oz (approximately 153yd/140m) per ball
- Recommended gauge: 28 sts and 38 rows to 4 in./10cm over St st using sizes 2–3 (2.75–3mm) knitting needles

YARN ADDRESSES

For the most successful results, use the yarn specified in your knitting pattern. Visit your local yarn shop or contact the distributors listed here for where to buy Rowan or Jaeger yarn near you.

USA
Westminster Fibers Inc., 4 Townsend West, Suite 8, Nashua, NH 03063
Tel: +1 (603) 886-5041/5043
E-mail: rowan@westminsterfibers.com

CANADA
Diamond Yarn, 9697 St Laurent
Montreal, Quebec H3L 2N1
Tel: (514) 388 6188

Diamond Yarn (Toronto)
155 Martin Ross, Unit 3
Toronto, Ontario M3J 2L9
Tel: (416) 736-6111
E-mail: diamond@diamondyarn.com
www.diamondyarn.com

STANDARD YARN WEIGHT SYSTEM

Categories of yarn, gauge ranges, and recommended needle and hook sizes from the Craft Yarn Council of America.
*Note: The following is a list of guidelines only. The information reflects the most commonly used gauges and needle or hook sizes for specific yarn categories.

Yarn weight symbol & category names	1 SUPER FINE	2 FINE	3 LIGHT	4 MEDIUM	5 BULKY	6 SUPER BULKY
Yarns types in category	sock, fingering, baby	sport, baby	DK, light worsted	worsted, afghan, Aran	chunky, craft, rug	bulky, roving
Knit gauge* in St st to 4 in.	27–32 sts	23–26 sts	21–24 sts	16–20 sts	12–15 sts	6–11 sts
Recommended metric needle size	2.25–3.25 mm	3.25–3.75mm	3.75–4.5mm	4.5–5.5mm	5.5–8mm	8mm
Recommended U.S. needle size	1 to 3	3 to 5	5 to 7	7 to 9	9 to 11	11 and larger
Crochet gauge* in sc to 4 in.	21–32 sts	16–20 sts	12–17 sts	11–14 sts	8–11 sts	5–9 sts
Recommended metric hook size	2.25–3.5mm	3.5–4.5mm	4.5–5.5mm	5.5–6.5mm	6.5–9mm	9mm and larger
Recommended U.S. hook size	B-1 to E-4	E-4 to 7	7 to I-9	I-9 to K-10½	K-10½ to M-13	M-13 and larger

Acknowledgments

Firstly, I'd like to thank Susan Berry, whose hard work, advice, and encouragement made creating this book a real pleasure!

I'm delighted with the way it looks, and for this I want to thank the following talented people—Nicky Downes, Sally Harding, John Heseltine, Emma Freemantle, and Penny Hill and Sharon Brant and their knitters.

Also I would like to thank the other designers who kindly allowed me to use their wonderful designs—Kim Hargreaves, Sharon Miller, Lois Daykin, and Martin Storey.